Welcome Home

written and illustrated by

Liz Cowen Furman

"But as for
me and my
household,
we will serve
the Lord."

Joshua 24:15

Traditions and Recipes that Say,

Welcome Home

All Year 'Round

written and illustrated by

Liz Cowen Furman

Honor Books is an imprint of
Cook Communications ministries, Colorado Springs, Colorado 80918
Cook Communications, Paris, Ontario
Kingsway Communications, Eastbourne, England

Printed in Korea.

1 2 3 4 5 6 7 8 9 10 Printing/Year 07 06 05 04 03

Editor: Julia Bates
Managing Editor: Janet L. Lee
Designer: Helen Harrison, YaYe Design
Design Manager: Jeffrey P. Barnes

This Welcome Home book is dedicated to the man without whom not one page would have been written. The inspiration for the book was his; many of the traditions and even recipes came from him and his family. The endless hours I spent drawing and writing this book took me away from the home (especially from the housework) and he pitched in to pick up the slack to help make a dream come true. He is the first to cheer me on and the last to doubt me. He is my most honest critic, our spiritual leader & he has a great sense of humor. He is an even better Dad to our boys than I imagined; a hopeless romantic, he is. . .

The Man of My Dreams!
The Honorable David M. Furman

The book is also dedicated to the three boys we love so much. I often marvel that God has given us not one, not two, but three of the most wonderful kids to raise for Him—**martin**, **matthew** and **micah**! These three also gave me endless support in the long book writing, drawing & painting process.

Note: It took a lot of folks to get this project to press, don't miss the acknowledgments in the back of the book.

Praise be to the God and Father of our Lord Jesus Christ, who has blessed us in the heavenly realms with every spiritual blessing in Christ.

Ephesians 1:3

That's Paul for, "Give God the Glory for Every Blessing!"

And whatever
you do, whether in
word or deed,
do it all in the name
of the Lord Jesus
giving thanks to
God the Father
through Him.

Colossians 3:17

I have a note above my drawing table that reads:
"Hey Liz! Remember to do all your work
as unto the Lord!" It helps.

Contents

Winter

Spring

Summer

Celebrating Autumn

Autumn—without a doubt my favorite season. Where I live in the foothills of the Rocky Mountains, the air grows crisp and the sunny afternoons end too soon. In the early fall, we wake up one day and it's as if overnight the aspen and cottonwoods decided to change clothes. For a few magical weeks they are dressed in finery of gold and yellow, auburn, and red. My family loves to walk the trails around our home. On windy days, with the sweet scent of damp leaves underfoot, it sometimes seems as if the whole sky is raining petals of gold.

Autumn is when my heart longs for the comforts of home. As the days grow chillier, home beckons ... snug slippers and a steaming mug of tea. Over the years, my family and I have discovered fun and meaningful ways to celebrate this colorful season of change. Together we have learned to build traditions and memories that, we believe, will last a lifetime.

I share these experiences hoping you will find special ways to commemorate this season, and all the others, with your family. The ideas in this book can be adapted easily to meet your family's circumstances. So, pick and choose. We don't even try to do all of these activities every year.

Each section of this book offers a few verses that have encouraged me along the way. As you read and plan new ways to connect with your family, I hope they will encourage you too.

From the time the world was created, people have seen the earth and sky and all that God made. They can clearly see his invisible qualities — his eternal power and divine nature...

Romans 1:20 (NLT)

a steaming mug of tea

When company arrives, make sure they know you were looking forward to seeing them. I keep poster board on hand so we can make a welcome sign at a moment's notice. I write big hollow letters for my kids—Martin, Matthew, and Micah—to color. Then we decorate the edges with stickers and pictures. The boys like to draw things the visitor likes. For Grammy and Papa, they draw bears. But if we don't know our visitors very well, the kids draw seasonal pictures. On the day our guests are to arrive we tape the sign to the front door. For extended stays we move the sign to our guests' bedroom door. Afterwards, we send the sign home with them. These mementos are always a big hit.

WELCOME JEFF & JENNIFER

The Apples of Autumn

Near my father's home on the western slope of Colorado, roadside stands sell fresh apples from the surrounding mountain orchards. Every fall we buy at least two bushels each of Jonathan, Gala, and Golden Delicious. Though it may sound like a lot of apples for a family of five, we don't waste any part of the bounty we bring home. Thanks to my whiz-bang apple peeler, a gift I received from my good buddy Charlene, the whole family can join the fun of apple preparations. We peel, core, and slice apples for a good part of the day. And, I must admit, there's a fair amount of tasting going on while backs are turned!

To save for potpourri concoctions, I freeze the cores and some of the peels in zip top freezer bags. Steeped with cinnamon, these "leftovers" make fragrant potpourri. All through the fall and winter, the aroma of apples fills our house. In winter, I add nutmeg and vanilla to the pot for a Christmassy scent. Pop a few frozen cores into water and simmer with spices. It's easy! (Keep an eye on your guests, though. They may try to drink your potpourri!)

Cheerfully share your home with those who need a meal or a place to stay.

1 Peter 4:9 (NLT)

One day I was boiling some old apple cores and peels left from the previous fall. I was experimenting to see if freezer burn diminishes their fragrance. (It doesn't.) Our youngest, Micah, flew into the kitchen and asked, "Oh mommy, is it fall? 'Cuz it smells like fall!" Micah had only lived four autumns and already he remembered that sweet smell and the season it represents.

With the apple slices, we make heaps of applesauce and yummy apple crisp. I also freeze some slices so that, when unexpected guests drop by, I can whip up a delicious dessert in minutes.

We want each person who visits our home to experience Christ's love in a real and tangible way. We want them to feel welcomed, cared for, and well fed.

Anyone can count the seeds
in an apple, but only God can
count the apples in a seed.
—Dr. Robert H. Schuller

Quick Apple Crisp

Preheat oven to 350°

7-10 apples, peeled and sliced—Granny Smith or Jonathan work well

1 box dry yellow cake mix

1 c. butter or margarine, melted

1/2 tsp. cinnamon

1/2 tsp. nutmeg

1/2 c. chopped pecans, walnuts, or almonds—optional but tasty!

Put apples into a cake pan sprayed with oil. (A glass pan works well.) Pour dry cake mix, mixed with nuts if using them, over apples, being careful to spread it evenly. Sprinkle cinnamon & nutmeg over cake mix & drizzle with melted butter. Bake at 350° for 45 minutes to 1 hour or until apples are bubbly hot & lightly browned on top.

This is great served warm with vanilla ice cream. As an added bonus, your kitchen will smell scrumptious.

Apples—

- Are high in fiber—about 5 grams each
- Suppress the appetite
- Fight viruses
- Lower cholesterol

- Prevent tooth decay
- Contain anti-cancer agents
- Help stabilize blood sugar

- Lower high blood pressure
- Prevent constipation
- Have anti-bacterial, anti-inflammatory & estrogenic properties

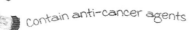

Apples—comfort food at it's best!

According to Healing Foods of the Bible and Food-Your Miracle Medicine the old adage, "An apple a day keeps the doctor away" might not be far off.

OFF TO SCHOOL

When Martin, our firstborn, started school, it finally dawned on me that I wouldn't always be with him to protect him. One would think that, as a former kindergarten teacher, I would have figured out that simple truth a little sooner. Though I'm really not an overprotective mom, when I finally realized my limitations it was like I had been hit by a ton of bricks. Who will defend my Martin from bullies? What if his teacher isn't nice to him? What if his classmates don't ask him to join them on the playground? Then my wise friend Cay told me that every morning she gives her children to God and thanks Him for the time they have had together. She asks His angels to guard over them and the Holy Spirit to lead, guide, and protect them.

Cay's words were an important reminder to me that God is in control, not me. Now I pray that same prayer every morning for my children and husband.

For God has not given us a spirit of fear, but of power and of love and of a sound mind. 2 Timothy 1:7 (NKJV)

I command you—be strong and courageous! Do not be afraid or discouraged. For the LORD your God is with you wherever you go. Joshua 1:9 (NLT)

School Supplies Shopping Spree

⭐ Shopping for school supplies is a grand event in our household. My boys and I pile in the car for an afternoon of important decisions—which colored pencils are the best? What's the coolest looking folder and the hottest style pencil box?

⭐ Be patient. Let your kids pick their own supplies. By allowing them the freedom to make choices, they'll have a sense of ownership about the things you buy.

⭐ Also, don't forget to write their names or initials on all their supplies with a permanent marker. I print out computer labels to attach their names to notebooks. I like to use a fun type style and include their teacher's name on the label.

After all the supplies are on board, we top off our shopping spree with an ice cream feast or one last summer frolic on the playground.

Homework

Dave and I believe that the children entrusted to our care must learn to do their very best. It's not enough to make good grades. We want our children to honor God with their words and actions. We want them to be lights to the world. We often talk with them about what this means.

In our house homework is serious business. Each kid was given a desk when he started in kindergarten, but often we end up around the dining room table together. It's easier to help everybody that way. By being involved in their studies, we show them that their education is important to us, too. In fact, everything we do around homework time helps to show each child how important he is to us, and how much we want him to succeed.

It's a good idea to volunteer in your child's classroom as often as possible. Not only is it a special occasion for the kids, but it's also very enlightening!

Whatever you do, work at it with all your heart, as working for the Lord, not for men.
Colossians 3:23

All about Me

What you make of yourself is your gift to God. What you are is God's gift to you.

Outside the Box
Lunch Ideas

Our seven-year-old seldom eats cafeteria food. For him, it's a sack lunch or starvation. Realizing how uninspired his lunches had become, I called 'all hands on deck' for a brainstorming session. The boys and I discovered many new (nutritious!) sack lunch ideas. We asked several friends to contribute to our list. My dear friend and pediatrician Jean also provided valuable input.

Fruits

Orange smiles
Mango chunks
Apples
Grapes
Banana
Kiwifruit—peeled & sliced

Dried fruit rolls—look for 100% fruit & avoid corn syrup
Frozen pineapple chunks or grapes
Strawberries
Fresh blueberries

Main Dishes

• Peanuts—if your school doesn't ban nuts • Cashews—Martin calls 'em "Moon Nuts"

• Small yogurts of any type • Cheese slices with crackers • Cubed cheese, string cheese,

American cheese slices • Cheesy tortilla—melt in microwave before putting in lunch box

• PB&J tortilla • Hard-boiled eggs (peeled) • Pepperoni—we always buy the turkey variety

• Turkey Bacon Jerky • Salami slices with crackers • Cheese crackers

Desserts

Homemade cookies (matthew says "Homemade is best!")

Fruit rings or chocolate cookie cereal—a few more vitamins

Caramel corn & cookies

Candy corn or a seasonal candy—jelly beans, candy hearts, Christmas ribbon candy

Jello with fruit on top

Fruit slices & chocolate spread, pudding, or peanut butter for dipping

Veggies

Carrots, broccoli, or other veggies & dressing for dip (Dip travels well in a zip top bag.)

Celery sticks stuffed with cheese or peanut butter

Chips–Baked potato, corn or veggie chips (Are chips veggies?)

Frozen peas and green beans–they'll thaw by lunchtime & keep the lunch cool

Black olives, cherry tomatoes, & pickles

Lunch Box Facts

Save take-out packages of mustard, ketchup, mayo, salt & pepper to add to lunch boxes.

If your kids won't drink milk plain, try sending chocolate or strawberry flavored powders in a baggie. They can mix it in the milk carton.

Remember those little ice packs that keep lunch boxes cool? Now they come in playful shapes. They're re-freezable & help to keep egg salad & other perishables cool until lunchtime.

Love Notes in a Sack Lunch

When I take time to write notes and hide them in sack lunches, my kids almost always come home reporting that the other kids wish their moms would do the same. Still, at a particularly tender age, one of our boys was embarrassed by the notes. I had to find another way to send him messages of love and encouragement. I once read a very clever tip. The writer suggested telling kids that the labels on fresh fruits and veggies, like "Dole" and "Sunkist," are really top-secret code words for "I love you!" I've practiced this clandestine form of communication for years now. Just one Chiquita Banana label on the sandwich bag and my son gets the message, and no one else has a clue.

We make our own valentines & I like to make a bunch of extras to use as gift tags (or to send) as notes to my kids, husband, teachers, & friends.

Before the rush of lunch making, cut several pieces of paper to keep in the kitchen near where you prepare lunches. Add a sticker or two to each note for decoration. Then in the morning, you can dash off a few words of love & tuck the note in the lunch box.

If your days begin in a flurry & you can't muster the energy to be creative at 7 a.m., stock up on Itty Bitty Notes from Ambassador. Our neighborhood Christian bookstore offers these wonderful little notes of encouragement for just a few cents. Our guys love 'em because the pictures are so funny. Recently, I discovered that they've kept almost all of the Itty Bitty Notes I've sent them. While cleaning one afternoon, I found their secret stashes ... stuck to the headboards of their beds!

Ideas to write on the notes:

- Study hard & have fun!
- Do your best!
- We believe in you!
- I am praying for you today! (Then do it.)
- Only 3 days left until Thanksgiving at Grandma's!
- Ace your test today!
- You are the one I'd choose.
- It's beginning to look a lot like Christmas!
- You are an amazing third grader!
- I love the way you helped clean out the garage this weekend!
- Jesus loves you & so do I!
- Always sign your notes "Love, mom." (Or some variation on that sentiment.)

THE CLEAN-UP BRIGADE

Each Furman—from the big to the small—learns to pull his weight when it comes to household chores. Every six months or so we gather 'round the dining room table for high-level negotiations to decide who will do what. That way, no one gets stuck on puppy poop patrol forever.

The jobs are age appropriate, but the first several times one of the kids attempts a new task, I work with him to teach him how to do it properly. In truth, when my boys were younger, it was far more work supervising the troops than doing it myself. But, I am happy to report, determination and perseverance have paid off. Martin, Matthew, and even 6-year-old Micah have (at last!) achieved a commendable level of proficiency in household chores & responsibilities.

Train a child in the way he should go, and when he is old he will not turn from it.

Proverbs 22:6

Having said that, I also must admit that some weeks everything seems to fall apart. Ah, well. The next week we just start over and try again. If parenting has taught me anything, it is to be flexible.

On the computer, I make a chart of everyone's weekly chores. I usually save the file so there is a record of who did what, and when. I glue the charts to foam core or poster board then mount the sign low on the wall in a prominent place, so everyone has easy access. It's a great reminder for all of us.

On the back of each chart, I glue magnets so that the kids can use magnets on the front side to mark off the jobs they have completed. For a giggle, dig through the junk drawer & see how many old realtor magnets you can find. I cut them into tiny squares & cover them with smiley face stickers. The kids use these to mark off what they have done.

Kids' Chores

- Unload dishwasher
- Load dishwasher
- Pick up bedroom
- Shoe patrol
- Put away clean clothes
- Clean out cars
- Practice piano
- Pick up stairway & hall
- Set table
- Homework
- Feed fish
- Make beds
- Vacuum
- Dust
- Pick up living room
- Pick up dining room
- Change oil with Dad
- Clean up whatever you got out of toy room
- Pick up hall & entry
- Feed & water dogs
- Feed & water bird
- Clear off table after dinner
- Clean off desk
- Clean out cars
- Empty trash cans
- Poop patrol

I am blessed with a husband who is actually better at cleaning than I am. Before we have guests over, everyone chips in. It's amazing how fast we can make the house shipshape when all hands are on deck!

Everyone in our family is responsible for carrying his or her own dishes to the kitchen after a meal. The kids are expected to ask to be excused and to thank the chef for the meal. Sometimes that thank you is offered with more enthusiasm than other times. Cheese pizza and Grammy's Jello salad never fail to win resounding appreciation.

The way Dave and I figure it, some day our boys will have wives (God willing!) who will appreciate such simple gestures of gratitude.

Incredible
Edibles

Prelude to the meal, appetizers are marvelous icebreakers. As guests congregate around the table to snack, the smiles & how-do-you-dos soon begin.

Mary Ellen's Crab Cakes
A winner at every gathering!

1—5 oz. jar Kraft Old English Cheese
   Spread
1/2 c. margarine
1 Tbsp. mayonnaise

1/4 tsp. seasoned salt
1/4 tsp. garlic powder
1—6 oz. can crab, drained
6 English muffins

Mix first five ingredients. Flake crab & add to mixture. Open muffins & cut each circle into quarters. Spread mixture on pieces. Place on cookie sheet. Bake at 400° for 10 minutes. This handy make-ahead recipe can be prepared & frozen up to two weeks in advance. Makes 48 crab cakes. Every time we get together with Mary Ellen we pray she'll bring this to the party. Scrumptious!

God is our refuge & strength, always ready

The Embellished Relish Tray

The relish tray—too often an overlooked treasure of savory and nutritious nibbles. Even the finicky eaters of the family (I won't point fingers!) like to sample from the relish tray. Some of the items I've suggested here are a bit pricey, but we go this flashy only a few times a year. Add or subtract items that appeal to your family's tastes, but be sure there are lots of colors on the tray.

     Sometimes we make a fruit tray and a veggie tray. In the center of the veggie tray, I put a pretty bowl filled with ranch dip mix and sour cream garnished with cilantro or parsley.

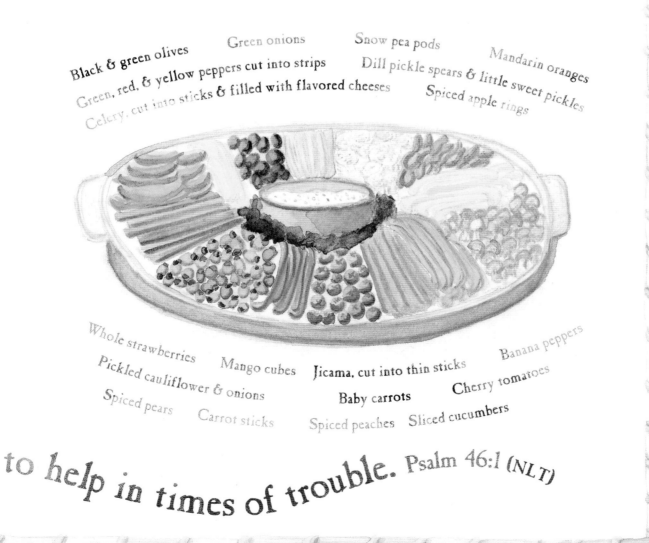

Black & green olives

Green onions

Snow pea pods

Mandarin oranges

Green, red, & yellow peppers cut into strips

Dill pickle spears & little sweet pickles

Celery, cut into sticks & filled with flavored cheeses

Spiced apple rings

Whole strawberries

Mango cubes

Jicama, cut into thin sticks

Banana peppers

Pickled cauliflower & onions

Baby carrots

Cherry tomatoes

Spiced pears

Carrot sticks

Spiced peaches

Sliced cucumbers

to help in times of trouble. Psalm 46:1 (NLT)

Decorating for WARM WELCOMES

As the season changes into fall, take time to notice. Ask yourself: What kind of God creates such a spectacle of color, intricate designs, & amazing life? He is the God who created you, too.

Hang grapevine wreaths full of interesting dried flowers, pods, & fall picks. What, you ask, are "fall picks"? Fall picks are small sticks with flowers, leaves, & seasonal decorations wired to them. They're used to decorate wreaths & flower arrangements. Most likely, you'll find them in craft stores. Look for them at half-price sales & stock up.

To make an autumn wreath—tuck a few fall picks in between a bunch of silk flowers & add a bonny bow for a focal point. If you're having a tough time tying the bow, not to worry. Just ask a crafty friend to help you. It's about a one-minute project for someone who's mastered the nimble-fingered art of bow tying.

While you're at it, make an extra wreath for someone who doesn't have time to make one. Leave it on their porch with an anonymous note saying "Happy Fall Y'all!"

I like to bring the colors of fall indoors. Around doorways—inside & out—on mantles & banisters, I drape silk garlands of auburn, red & gold leaves entwined with tiny white twinkle lights to give the room sparkle.

Find yourself an ample-sized horn of plenty. Line it with a pretty autumn napkin & fill with strange & wondrous gourds & petite pumpkins. Throw in a few real or silk mums. Allow them to spill onto the table around the opening. Bunches of mini Indian corn are interesting additions to the mix. As a centerpiece, a horn of plenty—or cornucopia, as it is sometimes called—is unbeatable. It's long lasting, eye-catching & relatively inexpensive. It also makes a thoughtful thank you gift for a special teacher or neighbor.

GIVE THANKS WITH A GRATEFUL HEART

PUMPKIN PLAYGROUND

Scatter pumpkins of various sizes & shapes around the house. Group in sets of three, placing the biggest to the rear & odd sizes on either side.

Paint a face on a pumpkin with acrylic paint. A circle or oval template makes a helpful guide. Dress up Mr. Pumpkin Head with a classy fedora or derby. Add a fall pick to the top & a bow to the brim. Voila! A fine howdy-do for your doorstep.

If you're an earnest gardener, fall is payoff time for all those hours spent on your knees in the dirt. Plant mums & zinnias. They last weeks in amply watered bouquets & are so bright & cheery. Add lemon-lime soda or a little sugar to the water to extend the life of the bouquet.

I almost always include the kids in decorating activities. However, occasionally, while they sleep, I gussy up the house in secret. It's such fun to watch when they emerge from their rooms in the morning. We add other decorations, a little at a time, for weeks, so the boys have a chance to participate.

Assemble a Harvest Gathering near your front door or in your front yard. It's a warm way to welcome home family and friends and share seasonal cheer with neighbors too.

Happy Harvest

WARM HOMECOMINGS

Autumn Outing

Pile the kids—big and small—into the car and gather up some neighbors and friends. It's time to head for the great outdoors. Where I live when the trees reach their peak fall color, that's the perfect time for a brisk walk and picnic. With the leaves crunch-crunching under our feet, we explore the mountain paths—telling favorite stories, singing (with great gusto), and enjoying our togetherness. It's an invigorating way to celebrate the season and build lasting memories.

Those who live at the ends of the earth stand in awe of your wonders. From where the sun rises to where it sets, you inspire shouts of joy.

Psalms 65:8 (NIV)

The best way to share our

Picnic Recipe

Chicken Salad with Moon Nuts

2 c. halved seedless grapes
(red, green, or mix)

2 c. salted moon nuts
(cashews!), halves

2 lbs. cooked & cut chicken meat

2 celery stalks, finely diced

3/4 c. mayo (we use light)

1/2 c. sour cream

1 Tbsp. white wine vinegar

1 tsp. dried dill (optional,
however, I love it)

In a plastic container that has a tight fitting lid, mix the chicken, grapes, cashews & celery. Set aside. In a small bowl, combine mayo, sour cream, vinegar & dill. Pour over chicken mixture & stir well. make this the day before & refrigerate overnight. Serve on deli rolls or croissants. A snap to pack for picnics!

If you live where bittersweet grows, praise the Lord & grab the garden shears! Look for the delicate orange berries of the bittersweet vine while on your walk. If you find some, snip a few twigs to make a simple wreath or add to a centerpiece. Oh, how I miss the lovely bittersweet that grew wild near my early childhood home in Eudora, Kansas.

Along the way, our gang likes to snack on a batch of homemade party mix. Sometimes, in a moment of reckless abandon, I throw calorie caution to the wind & add chocolate candies to the batch after it has cooled completely. Yum!

Pressed or dried leaves can be glued to the front of a card & highlighted with a sprinkle of glitter or gold paint. Send it to someone with a fall birthday or simply to say "hello"!

While on your picnic, gather a bagful of colorful leaves. When you get home, put the leaves in a flower press or between the pages of a book. After they have dried sufficiently, laminate one or two together, punch a hole & add a ribbon to make a keepsake bookmark for someone who shared the day with you.

Take lots of people pictures while on your outing. Then order double prints so you can share the memories with your picnic pals.

faith is to share our lives.

Family Prayer Time

Along toward bedtime in the Furman household, we congregate for a tradition we call Family Prayer Time.

One boy is dispatched to round up everybody. When guests are present, we invite them to join us if they would like. Often they sit in but don't pray aloud, which is perfectly fine.

We let one of the kids start. The first boy usually asks to hold something as he prays ... like a favorite bedtime buddy (stuffed animal). When he finishes praying, he passes the buddy to whomever he chooses, and that person is the next to pray. Around it goes, until everyone has a chance to lift up praises and concerns to God.

Every November we use this time for praise and thanksgiving. This works out well because right on the heels of Thanksgiving comes a period when we are inundated with messages designed to encourage our discontent, so that we'll buy more stuff.

Sometimes—especially when it is late—one person will pray for the group. And, when there has been discord in our home, we will confess our sins.

Dave and I do this, too. It is humbling to say before your children and God that you have used your words to hurt someone—that you lost control and became impatient. But when we confess our sins and humbly ask for forgiveness, we teach our children many important things. We teach them that everyone falls short sometimes. We teach them that by admitting our sins and asking each other for forgiveness, we can restore our relationships. And we teach them that by asking God's forgiveness, our sins are washed away.

martin loves his stuffed snake.

Dave encourages us to pray for specific needs, so we can see our prayers answered—and we do, over and over again. We also have had conversations about when God answers "No" or "Not yet." We learn a lot about what our kids are thinking. It has been so good for their growing faith ... and for ours.

After prayer, we read a story, learn a memory verse, and have Bible story time. On late nights we may let the other things lapse, but Bible story and Family Prayer Time are constants.

Don't worry about anything; instead, pray about everything. Tell God what you need, and thank him for all he has done. If you do this, you will experience God's peace, which is far more wonderful than the human mind can understand. His peace will guard your hearts and minds as you live in Christ Jesus.

Philippians 4:6-7 (NLT)

The purpose of prayer is not to change God, but to allow God to change us. It is to discover and do God's will, not to obligate Him to do ours. The purpose of prayer is that God's splendor will be displayed on earth as it is in heaven.

—Jennifer Kennedy Dean

micah collects turtles.

27

THANKSGIVING DAY

Succulent smells of culinary masterpieces browning in the oven ... George Winston and Peter Kater melodies floating through the morning ... orange, burgundy, brown, yellow, red–fall's finest hues brightening up the house ...

Since 1789, when George Washington wrote his Thanksgiving Proclamation, Americans have set aside one Thursday in November to render to God "our sincere and humble thanks for his kind care and protection of the people of this country." Washington's intention was that we "unite in most humbly offering our prayers and supplications to the Great Lord and Ruler of Nations...."

Praise the LORD. Give thanks to the LORD, for he is good; his love endures forever.

Psalm 106:16

For more than two hundred years, Americans have been participating in the time-honored tradition begun by our first President. We invite others to share in the feast, the bonds of friendship, and the time of prayers and thanksgiving.

This meal is a symbol of God's abundant provision. This gathering of friends and family is the symbol of God's invitation to all of us to become part of his family. This day of thanks is an acknowledgement of our love for each other and for our God.

...chips & dip ...warm laughs & the safe harbor of home ...Let us give thanks and praise!

homemade stuffing & mashed potatoes ...

the whoop & hurrah of parades & football games on TV... candy corn & nuts in the shell & chocolate...

TABLE SET FOR A FEAST

salad plate

place marker

water glass

stem glass

Don't worry if you don't have all this silverware. We only have one fork for each person and no one cares!

coffee cup

dessert fork
dinner fork
salad fork

soup spoon
teaspoon
dinner knife

I want the Thanksgiving table to be utterly irresistible. I like to use place markers for a personal touch and candles for a warm, shimmering ambience.

The first year that we hosted the feast, we invited twenty-three of our closest family and friends. We had lots of camaraderie, but little money. Still, I wanted everything to be perfect. On a whim, I went to the store to look for fabric for tablecloths. I ended up burrowing through the upholstery clearance bin, where I made a rare and valuable discovery: beautiful soft brown tweed flecked with all the colors of fall. I cut the cloth to fit our tables and have cherished these Thanksgiving tablecloths ever since.

That year, our friend's father, Chet, came bearing gifts of chocolate and flowers. It was the first time I had ever received a hostess gift. I was so flattered. From then on, whenever I'm invited to a dinner, I try to remember to bring flowers from the garden or a pumpkin from our patch ... just something special to say thank you for welcoming us.

We've been known to add to our guest list just minutes before we carve Turkey Tom. I like to make a few extra place markers so late arrivals will feel welcome. When someone calls to inquire if a last minute addition is acceptable, we consider it an honor... maybe even a personal appointment from the Savior.

Be not forgetful to entertain strangers: for thereby some have entertained angels unawares. Hebrews 13:2 (KJV)

A FLOCK OF TURKEYS

What You Will Need To Make A Gobbler Place Marker

1 tiny straw hat or pilgrim hat from the craft store—for added charm, glue tiny silk flowers on the brim

6 inches gold cord or ribbon to complement your tablecloth or dishes

4 inches brown pipe cleaner

1 inch red pipe cleaner

1/2 inch yellow pipe cleaner

2 lidded jiggle eyes, medium size

1 wooden skewer—cut 4 inches from sharp end

2 x 3 inch colored paper to complement your table

1 piece of white or light colored paper—use wavy scissors or a deckle cutter to trim to slightly smaller size than colored paper

2 Tbsp. m&ms or any candy you like

5 x 5 inch squares of tulle cut with pinking sheers or straight scissors

(Tulle netting comes in lots of colors so you can mix & match or go monochromatic.)

glue gun & glue sticks

calligraphy pen

Lay a square of tulle on a flat surface & drop a small handful of candy into the center. Pull the fabric up around the candy & tie with cord or ribbon. It might help to put a small rubber band on first to make it easier to tie a bow. Fluff out the ends of the tulle to resemble turkey feathers. Set aside.

Coil one end of the brown pipe cleaner to form a simple turkey head. The other end will be attached to the gobbler's body. Use the glue gun to attach eyes to the head. Poke the yellow pipe cleaner through the front coil to make a beak. Poke the red pipe cleaner through the bottom of the front coil to make a wattle. Glue hat to top of head. Poke the stem of the pipe cleaner head into the body of tulle.

Use the calligraphy pen to write a message and name on a piece of white or light colored paper. Glue that onto a piece of colored paper, placing the dull end of the skewer between the two layers to make a little sign. Stick the sign into the body of the turkey and PRESTO! A Gobbler Place marker. Once you've cut the pipe cleaners and tulle—and gotten into the groove—these take only about 3 minutes each to make.

gobble, gobble gobble, gobble, gobble gobble,   gobble, gobble gobble, gobble

31

Warm-ups for

When your Thanksgiving guests arrive, give them each a 3 x 5 inch card decorated with a fall sticker or two. Ask them to write down five things they are thankful for. The littlest guests can dictate theirs. Before saying grace, invite your guests to share what they wrote. Hearing how good God is to us is such a blessing. Ask your guests to sign & date their cards so you can keep them. Not only will you have a record of who shared the holiday with you, but you will also have a box full of blessings commemorating the occasion.

Thanksgiving 2002
1. My new faith
2. Opportunities New
3. Health
4. April
5. Family

Uncle Fred Struck

Giving Thanks

Dig out some poster board & gather the whole gang into the room to brainstorm. Ask everyone to tell what he or she feels grateful for. Start with the kids. Pretty soon even the oldsters lined up on the couch will be shouting out blessings. Write everything mentioned, no matter how trivial it may seem. Afterwards, hang the poster in the playroom for the duration of the holiday season. It will be a gentle reminder to stay focused on what you have & not what you want. Be sure to write everyone's name & the date on the bottom of the poster.

We Are Thankful 2003

Grandpa Glen, Grandma Dorothy & Grammie, Papa, Paul Thalos The Stewarts, D&3M& Jan Laman

At the start of the meal, pass around a basket of raisins, peanuts, butterscotch chips, or other tiny edibles. Instruct everyone to grab a few & pass the basket. When the basket has made its way around the table, invite each person to count his treats then give thanks for that many things. Our friends, the Covino's, introduced us to this wonderful tradition. Our kids loved it & we've done it every autumn since.

BUTTERSCOTCH
Crunchies

When I was in the seventh grade at Cañon City Junior High, we made Butterscotch Crunchies in home economics. The lesson: How To Use A Double Boiler. It's been a few years—ok, more than a few years—since that lesson. Somehow I managed to retain the lesson about double boilers, but I couldn't quite remember the recipe. Thankfully, I saw the same recipe one day in a cookbook compiled by Matthew's second grade class.

How to make a Butterscotch Crunchie...

1/2 c. peanut butter

1 small pkg. butterscotch chips—if you don't
    like butterscotch, use chocolate chips

1-12oz. bag dry oriental chow mien noodles

2 c. mini marshmallows

Melt peanut butter & butterscotch chips in a double boiler. Remove from heat. Add noodles then marshmallows. Stir gently until coated. Drop one spoonful at a time onto waxed paper then wait to cool. So easy & yummy! In spring it's fun to use Crunchies to make edible nests for jellybean eggs.

Prayer is the oil that takes the friction out of life.
—Unknown

PORCUPINES

This is an old favorite from my Canadian friend Verleen.

1 c. brown sugar

1 Tbsp. butter

2 eggs

1 c. chopped pecans or walnuts

1 c. chopped dates

4 c. shredded coconut

Cream butter & sugar, add eggs & beat well. Add nuts & dates. Mix thoroughly. Drop one spoonful at a time into a dish of shredded coconut. Roll into oblong shape. Bake at 350°F on greased cookie sheet until delicate golden brown.

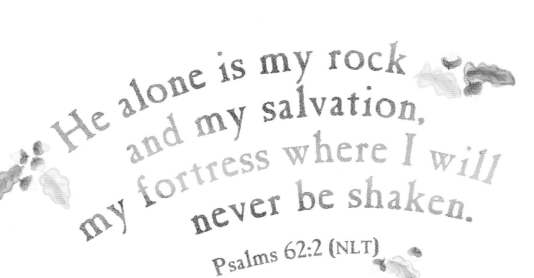

He alone is my rock and my salvation, my fortress where I will never be shaken.

Psalms 62:2 (NLT)

NEVER SAY LEFTOVERS!

Thanksgiving leftovers make up some of my all-time favorite meals. I can't understand why some folks duck and dodge when the day-old dressing and cranberry sauce come out. In case you have one of those types in your house, here are a few ideas to disguise the bird. My friend Lorri gave me these recipes years ago. She claims her husband Jerry would make this sandwich at the Thanksgiving table if she would let him. (She makes him wait till dinner's over.) My Dave loves this one, too!

Jerry's Broiled Turkey Sandwiches

1 loaf French bread	enough leftover turkey to cover bread
mayo	
1 can peeled, chopped green chilies—we like mild ones	cheddar cheese
	lettuce
	sliced tomatoes—optional

Cut French bread in half & lay open on cookie sheet. Spread mayo then chilies on one side. On the other side stack turkey & cheese. Broil in oven until cheese melts. Add lettuce & tomatoes, close bread, then cut into individual servings & dig in! This is great to serve the hungry hordes watching weekend football.

Lorri's Turkey Enchiladas

1 pkg. corn tortillas
3 c. leftover turkey, chopped
1 can enchilada sauce
1 large onion, diced

3 c. shredded cheddar (or other) cheese
guacamole, sour cream, chopped tomatoes & lettuce

Spray a frying pan with oil & lightly heat both sides of a corn tortilla. Dip in enchilada sauce. Put cheese & turkey into tortilla & roll into log. Make as many as you need & line up the tortilla rolls in a casserole dish sprayed with oil. Pour remaining sauce on top & sprinkle with cheese. Bake at 350°F until hot & bubbly, about 20-30 minutes.

Garnish with guacamole, sour cream, chopped tomatoes & lettuce. Olé!

Give us this day our daily bread.

matthew 6:11 (KJV)

37

Celebrating Winter

Winter is a magical time—bringing out the child in all of us whether we're 3 or 93. First, there is the wide-eyed anticipation of Christmastime with its sparkling lights and colorfully wrapped surprises. And don't forget the goodies from the kitchen! By the time the glitz and glitter of the New Year rolls around we're ready to look towards a new beginning with childlike faith. February rides in with Valentine's Day hearts ready to carry our messages of love to friends and loved ones. And, of course, there's chocolate! What would winter be without hot chocolate, baked chocolate, shaped chocolate, boxed chocolate—you get the idea.

Winter is the best time for reconnecting with loved ones near and far. It's a time of opportunity to reach out to those less fortunate than us. The wonder of winter warms the coldest of hearts!

One December it snowed a good foot the day before Grammy & Papa arrived from Wyoming. Not inclined to pass up a decent snowfall, the Furman gang wasted no time in donning mittens & parkas, mufflers & boots. Tromping into the snowy drifts, we set out on a mission to build snowboys that looked like our guys.

Martin's snowboy was the biggest; Matthew's was medium-sized; and Micah's was the smallest. The kids dressed the sculptures in their own snow gear & finished them off with oranges, carrots & other produce for eyes, noses & mouths. (Our neighboring deer & raccoons became fast friends to these frosty fellows!)

Afterwards we warmed our wet, frozen fingers around mugs of hot chocolate. When all fingers were back in working order, we penned welcome signs & hung them around the necks of our snow sculptures. Grammy & Papa were delighted.

Therefore, anyone who becomes as humble as this little child is the greatest in the Kingdom of Heaven.

Matthew 18:4 (NLT)

Auntie Zorah

Not everyone can boast of having an aunt with the name Zorah. She was a pearl beyond price. After my parents divorced, my sisters and I moved with mom across town just a few blocks away from Auntie Z's sunny yellow home.

I could easily walk to her cozy little place and felt drawn there many times a week. Because I visited so much, she told me "not to worry about knocking, just come in and give a shout." When I pushed open the front door, often the first thing I heard was the sweet sound of her deep vibrato voice singing "Amazing Grace," her favorite song. The vintage record player with its drop arm was stacked high with hymns that reflected her abiding faith.

I remember sitting for hours in her kitchen with its fire engine red ceiling and matching red vinyl diner chairs. The freezer at Auntie Z's was packed full of homemade cookies, and when I popped in for a visit she'd fix hot Tang® to drink and let me pick a bag of cookies to eat frozen.

She had many great adventures. My favorite Auntie Zorah story took place during a midnight blizzard on the eastern plains of Colorado. As a midwife, Auntie Z helped deliver my second cousin, who made his first appearance in the world a tad prematurely.

She knew he needed to be kept warm. So, right after his birth, she bundled him in a tiny blanket, tucked him in a shoebox, and placed the box on the open door of the oven. She then switched the oven on low and warmed him till he could hold his own.

The week of Christmas, Auntie Zorah would drive to our house in Leapin' Leena, her bright red station wagon. It was loaded down with a big box of homemade goodies. Auntie Z's arrival is one of my favorite Christmas memories.

I could write volumes about Auntie Z, but her cookie recipes are of heirloom quality, so I'll save room for a couple of them here.

Leapin' Leena

"The Lord has promised good to me,
His word my hope secures.
He will my shield and portion be,
As long as life endures."

...from Amazing Grace

Amazing Grace, how sweet the sound, that save a wretch like me.

Auntie Z's Fruity Cookies

(my kids rank these high on their list of favorites.)

3 c. flour	1 c. sugar
1 tsp. baking powder	1/2 tsp. salt
2-3 oz. packages dry Jell-O®	1 egg
(any red flavor)	1 tsp. vanilla
1 & 1/2 c. butter or margarine	

Mix flour, salt & baking powder together. Cream together butter, sugar & 1 package of Jell-O®. Add egg & vanilla & beat well. Shape into balls the size of small walnuts. Before baking, roll balls in second box of Jell-O® & smush flat with fork. Bake at 350° on ungreased cookie sheet just until edges begin to brown, about 10-12 minutes. (These cookies are better when they're soft, so watch closely to avoid overcooking.) I think I'll go make some of these ravishing red beauties right now!

These make great cookies for Valentine's Day, too. Make them heart-shaped and they'll be the favorites of the day.

Vanilla Wafer Date Cookies

1 lb. chopped dates	1 c. water
1 c. chopped nuts	2 boxes Vanilla Wafers
1/2 c. sugar	2 c. powdered sugar

Simmer dates, nuts, sugar & water in a pot on low heat until thick, 15-20 minutes. Cool & spread between 2 vanilla wafers. Roll in powdered sugar. If you prefer, substitute up to 1/2 of the dates with raisins. Store in a tightly sealed container. These freeze well but may need to be re-rolled in powdered sugar to look nice. When I make these cookies, I get visions of my childhood dancin' in my head.

I once was lost, but now am found. Was blind but now I see.

What is Christmas?

"Christmas is a time when some of our dreams come true."
—Grandpa Walton, from the Walton's Christmas Album

Christmas marks the time in history when God fulfilled our deepest dreams and needs. That feeling that something is missing in our lives is actually our basic need to be in relationship with our Creator, our heavenly Father. Nothing compares to the promise Christmas holds for those of us who believe. Nothing else fills this longing in our hearts.

Christmas is more than magical—it's miraculous! If Jesus had not been born, then He could not have died and paid the price for our sins. At Christmas we celebrate the greatest gift of all—Christ.

Personally, I love it that God chose to wrap His gift in strips of cloth...that His bed was a simple box of hay. It means a lot to me that the King of Heaven was born to a poor working family. His birth announcement may have been delivered by angels, but it was sent to shepherds not royals. Jesus' quiet, humble entrance speaks clearly to me of His love for all people everywhere—even me! Now that's something to treasure.

At our house the manger goes up first and comes down last every Christmas. My mom contends that Jesus was born in a cave. She builds the most magnificent cave stable every year. My feeble attempts to carry on this legend have become tradition at our house. By putting up the manger before any other Christmas decorations, we emphasize whose birthday we are celebrating. One year when our children were very young, everybody in the house was sick (Ever had one of those holidays?), we never got the tree decorated, but our manger stood as a comforting reminder of God's gift to all of us.

All who heard the shepherd's story were astonished, but Mary quietly treasured these things in her heart and thought about them often. Luke 2:18-19 (NLT)

42

How to build a cave manger scene...

On the table where you want the display, stack a few large books then drape a brown sheet over them. This will be the floor of the cave. To make the backdrop for the scene, find a sturdy piece of cardboard & cut into half an oval. For a reusable display, you might want to use a piece of plywood. On the backdrop, drill or poke holes in a random arch around the edge. Cover the curved board with shiny navy blue or starry night sky wrapping paper & poke holes in the paper to correspond with the holes in the board. Insert tiny white lights in the holes. Cut a star from white paper to attach high in the sky for the wise men to follow. (We also include the angel martin made in pre-kindergarten.)

backdrop with light holes

Crumple enough brown packing paper to arch over the backdrop. The crumpled paper represents the cave walls & ceiling. Staple the paper around the curved edge of the backdrop. Staple the bottom edges to the brown sheet. Scatter bits of straw around the floor of the scene.

Arrange mary & Joseph & a lamb on the top of the book pile & leave a space in front for baby Jesus. (Through the years all sorts of animals have appeared in our scene—elephants, turtles & my personal favorites: plastic bugs & fish.) We finish the scene with baby Jesus in the manger...but not until Christmas morning or late on Christmas Eve. One year Santa tucked Him in when he came to drop off the presents.

mom's magnificent masterpiece!

What must it have been like for mary? I've often wondered!

43

Matthew's Holiday Wreaths

Kids love to be involved in holiday preparations. When it's Matthew's turn to make evening snack for the family, these crunchy-chewy treats are often his choice. Here's his holiday version:

1/2 c. butter or margarine

1 pkg. 10 oz. large marshmallows
(need 40)

green food coloring

6 c. cornflakes cereal

cinnamon candies & red string licorice

In a large saucepan, melt butter over low heat. Add marshmallows & cook, stirring constantly until marshmallows melt & mixture is syrupy. Remove from heat & quickly stir in green food coloring. Carefully add cereal & stir until thoroughly coated. Allow the mixture to cool enough to handle safely. Using buttered fingers, quickly shape the cereal mixture into small wreaths & set them out to cool on wax paper. Adorn each wreath with cinnamon candies & a tiny licorice bow. Festive & delicious.

Variations

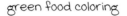

For one large wreath, pour the whole batch into a greased bundt pan & allow to cool. Then cut into single serving slices.

We've shaped the cereal mixture into green shamrocks, orange pumpkins, red Valentines' hearts & even brown teddy bears dressed in vests cut from blue Fruit Roll-ups®. A large cookie cutter sprayed with oil makes a great pattern to fit the occasion.

44

Matthew never learned to walk. He hit the ground running and has never slowed down since. For all of his energy, he often surprises us with the depth of compassion he shows for others. It's matthew who poured out the entire contents of his piggy bank to send to Grandma when her house needed a new foundation. It's matthew who makes sure nobody is left out when teams are picked at school. It's matthew who prays every night for his friends' salvation. And it's matthew who teaches us to be bold in our faith.

Sons are a heritage from the LORD, children a reward from him.

Psalms 127:3

Gingerbread– A Cottage Industry

The first year we hosted a gingerbread party, I planned it for the kids. I thought they'd get a kick out of decorating their own gingerbread house. When the kids finished their houses and tired of sneaking samples, I talked the adults into trying their hand at gingerbread building. After some initial resistance, the parents rolled up their sleeves and dove in.

The results were amazing: Dave made a fort guarded by gummy bears and pretzel cannons, another dad made Noah's ark with frosted animal crackers boarding two-by-two, and others have made their own ideas of sweet real estate. There's no doubt about it, adults enjoy this cottage industry just as much as kids do! And the creations get better every year. It is easy to throw a gingerbread bash and fun is guaranteed.

How to Throw a Gingerbread Party (for 20 or so friends)
Frosting for the House

2 lbs. powdered sugar	4-6 egg whites	1/2 tsp. cream of tartar

If you are using a hand-held mixer, start with 4 egg whites. Otherwise, use 6 egg whites. Mix the ingredients together at low speed until the powdered sugar stops flying. Then mix at high speed for 7-10 minutes. Frosting is done when mixture thickens and soft peaks form.

The night before your party, mix 3 batches of frosting. (Make one bowlful at a time because it hardens so fast. You won't need to wash the bowl between batches if you make them back-to-back.) Before the frosting has time to dry out, spoon about three tablespoons of it into small, zip top plastic bags. Zip closed & refrigerate until party time. The frosting will keep a long time if the bags are tightly closed. As you hand out bags to your gingerbread architects, snip one corner & voilà! A professional cake-decorating bag.

Make enough so that each person has 1-2 bags of frosting. One year, I dramatically underestimated the amount my builders needed. I spent a few frantic minutes during the party measuring, mixing & missing out on the fun.

If you're worried about the raw eggs in the frosting, tell the kids (and adults) that the frosting is like cement—it's not for eating. Or use powdered egg whites mixed with water as directed on the container.

On your invitations, ask everyone to bring a box of graham crackers. We use them instead of gingerbread and no one seems to mind that we didn't spend days baking the real thing. Also, ask them to bring 1-2 items to use & share as decorations: Christmas ribbon candies, pretzels, gummy bears, rope licorice, chocolate Kisses, cereals & any other small goodies. Cereals make great shingles & walkways.

A few days before the party, I go to the school cafeteria & rescue milk cartons from the trash or you can use 1/2 pint cartons for cream. I wash the cartons well & use them as bases for the graham crackers. Be sure to get plenty of cartons because some architects use more than one. Staple the tops closed for a better roof foundation. A bit of frosting will hold the crackers on the cartons.

To start a snow-white foundation for your builders, cut squares of cardboard from sturdy boxes & wrap the squares in freezer paper. In a pinch, sturdy white paper plates work fine.

Fill your house with great Christmas music to set the mood. We love classical versions of old favorites.

Save all that picked-through candy from Halloween and birthday party bags! A gingerbread workshop is a great place to unload it.

Some years, before the workshop opens, we serve kid-friendly hors d'oeuvres—veggies & dips & chili & corn bread. (A feeble & largely ineffective attempt to reduce candy consumption....)

We were filled with laughter, and we sang for joy. And the other nations said, "What amazing things the Lord has done for them."

Psalms 126: 2-3

47

Good Gifts

Every Christmas, my gift list out-stretches my pocketbook. Over the years, though, I've learned that if I'm willing, there are many ways to be penny-wise. The key is to show that you care about someone's needs and that you value the relationship. Here are a few ideas that might help.

Surprise someone by painting a room that needs it. A few years ago when my in-laws Muff & Mel came to Denver for a meeting, I went up to their motel to run the business in their absence. In the week they were gone, I painted their kitchen. It was one of those things that had been bugging Muff for a while, but persistent arthritis kept her from doing the job herself. You should have heard the shrieks of joy coming from that woman when she saw what I had done! A simple thing like painting a room—one would have thought I painted a whole nine-story castle, the way she carried on.

Give spring flower bulbs. In late fall you can get them for a song. Better yet, give them to a friend with a note offering to plant them in early spring. One year I bought a barrelful of bulbs on clearance & used them for stocking stuffers for school bus drivers, teachers, neighbors & Boy Scout leaders. It felt so good being able to shower gifts on so many when I had room in my budget to give to so few.

Every year Dave's dad—affectionately known as Papa—gives a special ornament to each of his kids' families. He pens tiny notes for each one commemorating current events, milestones, and special family memories from the year and puts the note inside the ornament. Both his notes and the ornaments are a part of our family history. For example, a few years ago he gave us a golf shoe ornament in honor of cousin Jonathan's golfing success. In his unique way, Papa is inscribing our most cherished family memories on our Christmas trees and leaving a legacy for our children.

Give chocolate. I don't think I need to elaborate on this one.

Peach Spiced Tea

make peach spiced tea mix & deliver it in a canning jar with a pretty ribbon & directions for brewing. Cover the top of the jar with bright Christmas fabric.

1 c. powdered Tang®
1/2 c. instant unsweetened tea
1/2 tsp. cinnamon
1/2 tsp. ground cloves

1 c. sugar
1/2 tsp. finely grated lemon peel
3 small pkgs. peach Jell-O®

Combine all ingredients in a bowl & mix well. makes 3 cups of tea mix. Directions for brewing: Add 2 Tbsp. to 8 oz. of boiling water & enjoy!

Buy a calendar & write all the family birthdays & anniversaries on it. April, my sister-in-law, made one for me & it was the only year I sent all the birthday cards on time. For the whole year, every time I looked at it, I thought of her.

Make a spring wreath & give it at Christmas as a symbol of welcoming the New Year.

Give a night-light to a little friend who needs a bit of reassurance at bedtime.

Make a certificate for free lawn mowing, snow shoveling, window washing, or trash taking out. Discover your loved one's least favorite chore & promise to do it for a month. (Then follow through!)

Give a journal & start it off with a collection of meaningful quotes & verses. Include those you think would inspire & encourage the receiver.

Enlarge & frame a terrific picture of something or someone the receiver loves.

Presents with Pizazz

A thing of beauty is a joy forever. –John Keats

Christmas gift wrapping has taken on a whole new meaning as our boys have grown. When they were small, Dave and I hid all the gifts to wrap until Christmas Eve. After the sandman arrived for the kids we would brew some tea or coffee and sneak down to the basement. The first order of business was tuning in a radio station that played Christmas music all night—then we dove in. Paper flew in all directions and we had a blast creating memories not only for our little ones but for us as well!

Now we include the kids in the process, especially in the wrapping of gifts they have chosen for loved ones. Dave and I still keep our basement date but the number of gifts we wrap has definitely decreased as the boys take responsibility for their own creations. They are also learning that love can go into the wrapping as well as the present.

Here are a few of the things that have worked for us to encourage the kids to make gift wrapping a part of their gift-giving experience.

Wrap packages in plain tissue paper, hand the kids some markers and stickers and turn them loose. The results are elaborate, interesting, and beautiful works of art.

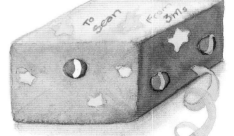

Purchase plain brown or white bags with handles. Pull out the stamps or paint and sponges with Christmas themes. Patterning is something even preschoolers can get into. Add a color coordinated sheet of tissue paper to the inside and you have a beautiful yet inexpensive gift wrap.

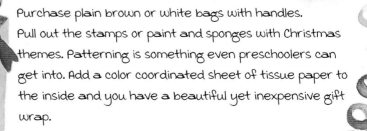

Don't forget the ribbon! my mom is the curly ribbon queen and I confess, I love it too! Curly ribbon is inexpensive and comes in every imaginable color. Wrap the gift in ribbon like usual, then add a 'bouquet' of curls in matching colors. Tie or tape in a Box Topper for some added pizazz. It's easy! It's festive! And the kids love it too!

Box Toppers

candy canes

small toys or keepsakes

jingle bells

To Seth

star cut-outs

cinnamon sticks

cookie cutters

small candles

ribbon candy

pine cones and sprigs

...but the gift of God is eternal life in Christ Jesus our LORD.
Romans 6:23

51

Christmas Eve

"Christmas. . .heaven at last for all of us!"
—Charles Dickens

These days not many traditions are carried down from generation to generation. But I'm happy to say, we're hanging on to one tradition that began at least two generations ago in Dave's family. Dave's parents and both sets of his grandparents read the story of Christ's birth on the eve of Christmas.

We start the festivities with a church service then head home for take-and-bake pizza and a salad...or some other no-hassle meal. Afterwards, Dave's dad blends a batch of eggnog and as we sip we cozy-up around the Christmas tree and manger.

As our kids get older, the responsibility of reading the Bible story is bestowed on them as a coming-of-age gift. The chosen reader practices for days beforehand. Dave still remembers when, at about 8 or 9, the torch was passed to him. After listening to the historical account of Christ's birth (in Luke, chapter 2), we sing our favorite old carols. I'll admit I'm sometimes off-key, but there's no doubt about the emotion that stirs in my heart as I listen to my family sing "Silent Night."

To end the caroling, we send up a rousing rendition of "Happy Birthday" to Jesus and then dive into the birthday cake. After the celebration, the kids choose one gift from under the tree to open. Then we put out cookies for Santa and the kids jump into bed.

"I bring you good news of great joy that will be for all people."
Luke 2:10

Happy Birthday Jesus!!

Happy Birthday to Jesus . . .

When our family was young and money was harder to come by, we informed the boys that they could ask Santa for only one present. Now we don't have to worry as much about money, but we've decided that the "One Gift from Santa" standard is a good one. Our boys receive many more than one gift each Christmas. We know their passions, but Santa only brings one present. He has so many kids to make gifts for, after all. He also fills their stockings to bursting. This tradition helps all of us take our eyes off the gifts & focus on the reason for the season.

Cheers!

Furman Family Eggnog

3 eggs
2 cans Eagle Brand® condensed milk (must use Eagle Brand®)
2 Tbsp. vanilla

1/2 c. white sugar
2 qts. regular milk
1 pint whipping cream

In a bowl, combine the eggs, condensed milk, vanilla & sugar & gently beat. Add milk & stir. In a separate bowl, beat whipping cream. When cream is fluffy, set aside a small amount to garnish each serving & fold the rest into the eggnog mixture. Pour into Christmas mugs or festive stemware & sprinkle with a dash of nutmeg & a dollop of whipped cream squirted from a pastry bag. Makes a little more than 2 quarts of good cheer.

♪ Happy Birthday to You! ♪

Christmas Morn

As a child, I could never understand why mom and dad were such sleepyheads on Christmas morning. Now, as a parent with three young boys, I have joined the ranks of the bleary-eyed. (Despite heroic attempts to get everything done before midnight.) Yet even in my sleep-deprived state, I can't believe the joy it gives me to watch our kids' faces as they peer at the gifts under the tree. It's as though their smiles and delighted squeals transport me back to my childhood Christmas mornings.

When I was a babe, my parents gave the countdown and my sisters and I tore into the gifts all at once. Dave's family takes a different approach. Once I adjusted to it, I came to love it. Nevertheless, I do feel there are merits to both plans of attack.

Here's how it works. As Christmas music drifts through the room, the boys sort and hand out the packages. Then, one at a time, starting with the youngest, the opening begins. It's great fun seeing what everyone receives and their reactions. The smallest in the group can play with their gifts while the older ones carry on with the opening. The result is a lovely, relaxed family time punctuated by a few good laughs when we open Papa's goofy gag gifts.

Everyone gives a gift to Jesus, too. We write what we will give Him on cards and wrap them. Since He is the oldest, we open and read His gifts last.

Dear Jesus, 2003
For Christmas for you we bought presents for the family we adopted through Angel Tree. Love, Martin

54

"The virgin will be with child and will give birth to a son, and they will call him Immanuel" —which means, "God with us."

matthew 1:23

Nutritional fortification for this important day traditionally begins with homemade cinnamon rolls, milk, juice, and, of course, COFFEE. (Not necessarily in that order.) Some years we splurge and buy fancy cinnamon rolls from the bakery.

We have discovered that what matters about family traditions is the sense of familiarity and comfort they give us. Whether our traditions are store-bought or homemade, the mere act of repeating them year after year is what builds that feeling of community and family that we long for.

Sharon's Caramel Cinnamon Rolls

- 2 loaves frozen bread dough
- 1 & 1/2 c. brown sugar
- 1 c. butter
- 2 Tbsps. light corn syrup
- 2 tsp. ground cinnamon (to taste)
- 2 Tbsp. flour—for keep dough from sticking to rolling surface

Thaw 2 loaves frozen bread dough in wrapper until soft enough to shape. To make caramel, combine 1 c. brown sugar, 1/2 c. butter & corn syrup in pot. Heat & stir until bubbly. Pour into 9" x 13" pan. Melt remaining butter in a separate container & set aside. On a floured flat surface, roll out each loaf of dough to about 8" x 12" Over each square, brush on half of melted butter then top with 1/4 c. brown sugar & 1/2 tsp. cinnamon. Roll tightly to make 12" logs. Slice logs into 1" thick rolls & place on top of caramel. Cover pan & let dough rise in a warm place till doubled in size (about 30 mins. to an hour). Preheat oven to 375°. Bake uncovered for 15-20 mins. or until light brown. Cool 2-3 mins. then invert pan of rolls onto serving platter. Hint: use a platter with an edge—these are gooey, messy & finger-lickin' good!

A Place for Everyone at the Christmas Table

The Christmas table is all about sparkle! While I might dress up the table a little differently every year, my main hope is that everyone remembers the glow of warmth that comes from not only our table, but our home and family as well. If you're looking for something easy to make, Christmas ball ornaments are great place markers. Afterwards, guests can take them home as keepsakes to remember where they were on Christmas day and with whom they shared the celebration.

All the things you'll need to make Christmas ball place markers—

one glass ball ornament for each person at your table—
choose colors to complement your table settings
a gold or silver pen
enough ribbon to make a bow for each ball
small rubber bands—one for each ball

On each ball, write the name of a guest, your family name, and the year.

On the other side of the ball, write a Christmas message:. Tie a tiny bow around the top & set the ball on a small rubber band to prevent it from rolling around the table.

BEN 2003

For unto you is born this day... a Savior who is Christ the Lord.

Annette, my good friend, recently asked me to recreate a Christmas ball I made for a party we had one year. Hers accidentally broke and she said her tree wouldn't be complete without it.

56

Then make me truly happy by agreeing wholeheartedly with each other, loving one another, and working together with one heart and purpose.
Philippians 2:2 (NLT)

Center of Attention Centerpieces

Good table manners. A tall, bushy centerpiece ruins the conversation. A good guide is to make it less than 12" or 14" high. Narrow candles or spires taller than that won't be a problem, but the bulk of the decoration should sit below eye level.

Ever-ready evergreens. If you live where evergreens grow, cut a few choice sprigs of juniper, holly, or pine for your table. Before you arm yourself with the clippers, though, there are a couple of important considerations. First, never cut branches within range of four-legged critters whose job description involves marking territory. Second, always give greens a good shake to discourage

buggy guests from attending your dinner.

Simple essentials. Set a candle in the middle of a spray of evergreens. For a lighthearted, cheery touch, tuck a few knickknacks or small Christmas picks into the greens & add a bow or two. I always sprinkle tiny gold stars around the table to give it that glittering effect. If you're having many guests and the table is long, repeat the arrangement several times.

Light up the room. Whatever you do, light plenty of candles. Softly flickering candlelight is a sure sign something special is happening.

Borrow from your tree. Show off your treetop angel or favorite ornaments by using them as table decorations. Or, enlist the nativity characters to pose in the center of the table amongst the bows, greens & candles.

Heedless of the Wind & Weather, Fa-la-la-la-la, La-la-la-la!

Who can resist the thrills & spills of sledding! If you're too tender to hop on, be sure to take time to watch. Then warm up with these family favorites.

Praise the Lord for instant hot chocolate—it's so easy. Much as I like to cook, it's hard to beat the convenience of ready-made. If it gets a little too hot, pour in a splash of real milk to cool it down. Milk makes the chocolate taste richer & the kids won't scald their tongues. Don't forget to bring on the marshmallows or a dollop of squirty whipped cream from a can. What could be more wonderful than hot cocoa on a frosty afternoon?

There is a time for everything, and a season for

Snowball Crunchies

I c. softened butter

I Tbsp. vanilla

1/4 c. white sugar

1/4 c. powdered sugar

1 c. chopped pecans (optional)

2 c. sifted flour

Mix butter, vanilla & white sugar until creamy. Add nuts & flour. Pinch off dough & roll into ping-pong ball-sized snowballs. (About 1 inch.) Bake at 300 for 35-40 minutes or until brown. While still warm, roll in powered sugar. Crunch away!

Hot Chocolate Mix

(Homemade instant mix that's lots yummier than store-bought.)

1 – 8 qt. box powdered milk (10 2/3 c.)

1/2 lb. powdered sugar (1 § 3/4 – 2 c.)

6 oz. powdered coffee creamer

1 lb. instant chocolate milk mix

Combine all ingredients § mix well. Divide into smaller portions § distribute jars of mix as gifts to those you love. Include directions:

Stir 1/3 cup of mix into 2/3 cup boiling water. Sit by the fire § sip.

Before pouring in the hot liquid, put a peppermint disc in the bottom of the cup ...or a chocolate mint patty... or give a peppermint stir stick. Very festive!

every activity under heaven.
Ecclesiastes 3:1

Hippo Bakery Pecan Pie
(straight from heaven!)

In the early 80's, there was a small pastry shop in Las Animas, Colorado, called The Hippo Bakery. The smells that rushed out of the door when my sister Paula and I entered made us delirious. I, being a self-professed pecan pie connoisseur, felt it my duty and obligation to test the pecan pie from this little shop. Without a doubt, it was the best I'd ever put in my mouth! Sadly, the Hippo Bakery is no longer in business. The owners, however, were kind enough to share their superb recipe with me. My sister Jane and I make this pie every Christmas and Thanksgiving...and sometimes in between!

Pie Crust

1/2 c. butter

1 c. flour

1/2 tsp. salt

3-4 Tbsp. icy-cold water

Cut butter into flour. Add salt & water. Mix well until dough forms a large ball. On flour-dusted surface, roll out dough to fit a 9" pie pan. Crimp edges between fingers to make a fluted edge.

Pecan Filling

1 c. sugar
3/4 c. light corn syrup
1/2 c. butter
3 eggs

1 c. chopped pecans—I leave some whole, too. (Sometimes I add a few extras 'cause I'm a nut!)
1 tsp. vanilla

Blend sugar, syrup & butter then cook over medium heat. Stir until mixture boils. In a second, larger pan, beat eggs. Remove the hot mixture from the stove & slowly whisk it into the eggs. Stir in the pecans, then vanilla. Pour mixture into a 9" pie pan lined with crust. Bake at 375° for about 45 minutes. To catch syrupy drippings & cut down on mess, put a cookie sheet one rack below the baking pie.

Do not even try to double this recipe. The pecans rise in the syrup & it's nearly impossible to divide the mixture into two even pies. I tried it one Thanksgiving Eve & regretted it!

May the God of hope fill you with all joy and peace as you trust in him, so that you may overflow with hope by the power of the Holy Spirit.

Romans 15:13

The Royal Treatment

When I was a third grader at Lincoln Elementary in Cañon City, Colorado, my teacher told us to put our proper names on our Valentine's bags. The kids in my class urged me to write "Queen" in front of my name. I did so and, for one fleeting day, I became Queen Elizabeth. That was more years ago than I care to count and it's still such a sweet memory.

Everyone deserves the royal treatment once in a while and Valentine's Day seems especially suited for it.

For a couple weeks prior to Valentine's Day, drop a handful of candy hearts into a loved one's lunch box.

Send your child's teacher a big-hearted Valentine. February is a long month for those who not only impart knowledge, but also must ward off the pandemonium threatened by cooped-up kiddos jazzed on sugar.

Sprinkle tiny metallic hearts in unexpected places throughout the house.

Ever wonder what people do with those delicate white doilies? Why not dress up your plain valentines for an old-fashioned look? Glue your child's photo to the center of a matted doily. Decorate with sweetheart stickers & have your child sign & date the back. Slide it in an envelope, seal it with a kiss & send it to someone who will treasure it.

Surprise the ones you love. Write notes of appreciation & encouragement to everyone in the family & squirrel the notes away in sock drawers, under pillows, behind toothbrushes, in a shoe, or on the breakfast plate. They're sure to find several on Valentine's Day, but some may remain undetected for days...even better to find an unexpected love note on an ordinary, humdrum Tuesday.

Be sure your children see you & your spouse exchanging valentines. Even if it is just a card, these thoughtful gestures show our children what love-in-action looks like.

Live a life filled with love for others, following the example of Christ, who loved you and gave himself as a sacrifice to take away your sins. And God was pleased, because that sacrifice was like sweet perfume to him.

Ephesians 5:2 (NLT)

Ideas for Love Bugs

Love can change humbugs into hugbugs. Here are some fun and easy gift ideas to shower your friends and family with love.

Handprint hugs. Dip your little one's hands in watercolor paint then press her open palms onto white paper. Trim around handprints. Trace both outlines on card stock & trim slightly outside lines so that these mats are larger than the handprints. Glue one print to each mat. Punch a hole in both mats. Tie one end of a 25" ribbon to one handprint & the other end of the ribbon to the other print. And there you have it—a hug to keep forever. Eight years ago my mom received one of these hugs from her granddaughter, Jo. To this day, it hangs on the door to Grandma BJ's craft room.

Potato prints. Carve cold raw potatoes & sponges into smooches & hearts & then use them to stamp cards.

"I have loved you, my people, with an everlasting love. With unfailing love I have drawn you to myself."

Jeremiah 31:3 (NLT)

Be bold. Emboss. You'll need an embossing heat gun, valentine stamp, embossing inkpad & powder. Press stamp onto pad & then onto card stock. Sprinkle powder over design. Gently tap excess off card & then melt with heat gun. martin loves to make cards this way. It's easy, but adult supervision is a must; that gun gets hot!

Attach a treat. Have I mentioned chocolate lately? Even a plain valentine looks turned out with a tasty treat attached.

Bookmarks for book lovers. So easy for kids to make. Trim card stock to bookmark shape & stamp on the recipient's name in fancy letters.

Remember the bus driver; librarian; gym, art & music teachers; co-workers; next-door neighbors & elderly friends. A little valentine that takes just a few minutes to put together can bring joy for months to come.

Rosebud Kisses

green floral stick
pink or yellow plastic wrap
2 chocolate kisses, glued bottom to bottom
silk rose leaves
Wrap kisses in small squares of plastic wrap and secure. Mount kisses on floral stick and attach leaves. Starting at the flower base, wrap down stick with floral tape. Finish off with ribbon or a bow.

Celebrating Spring

ahh...fresh air!

I can't wait to throw open the doors and windows on a warm day to breathe in the sweet freshness of spring. So many times on a rainy day in April, I'll stop and savor that wet earth aroma and marvel at what a great Creator we have. He blesses us constantly with his creations.

There are many things in life that will catch your eye, but only a few that will grab your heart. Pursue those.

Words of wisdom from my friend Steve Sperry.

When my little one races in our front door shouting, "mom, your garden has flowers!" I know that spring has sprung.

I look forward to that special day when tiny yellow crocuses pop through the ground. We usually have our biggest snowfalls in March, but once Valentine's Day is over, I'm ready for spring. Seed catalogues call out to me. I yearn for trips to the local greenhouse. It's as if the earth begins to yawn and stretch and wake up for another exciting season.

As a teacher I loved to take my kindergarten class students out of doors to 'find' spring. The best time for our neighborhood jaunts was right after a Springtime shower. The kids were so excited to spy a robin building her nest or to watch the wiggly worms on the sidewalk. They were delighted to discover a tiny plant poking its head through the dirt or spot a bud bursting open. Is there anything as delicate as those first transparent light green leaves we've waited so long to see?

Once I brought a fluffy baby lamb to school to visit for a day (and my name's not even Mary)! I so enjoy using the springtime miracles of new life to sharpen the observation skills of children. Now it is my own children who saunter forth in search of spring and I love it all the more.

Spring brings energy and renewal—a sense of anticipation for new things to come.

Bring in the Spring!

Spring, like fall, offers wonderful natural resources for dressing up your home.

Gather baskets of all sizes & fill them with pots of spring blooming bulbs. When the flowers are spent, plant the bulbs outside for next spring's outdoor display.

Our kids receive resin figurines in their Easter baskets every spring. We use the previous years' collections to decorate the house. On the bottom of each figurine, I write the child's name & the year, so that when they start a family (God willing), they'll have some childhood mementos to use as decorations.

Colorful bouquets of cut flowers—they're the most wonderful way I can think of to bring spring indoors. I set flowers here & there throughout the house. Some of my favorites are Peruvian lilies or Alstroemeria. They're inexpensive, come in a variety of shades— yellow, gold, apricot, blushing pink & red. Best of all, they last up to 3 weeks in a well-tended vase.

To add a touch of class to a simple arrangement, try scouting through cabinets to find a unique piece that can substitute as a vase—delicate crystal creamers or tiny serving cups look lovely holding small bouquets.

The Lord lives! Blessed be my rock! May the God of my one of my favorite Easter verses.

DECORATIONS POLICE

Start a collection of wreaths for every season. It's an easy way to keep pace with the changing times & kids love them. If I don't put up the next holiday wreath soon enough, I'm sure to receive notification about it from a member of the Decorations Police. (They're an observant bunch.)

Find a large clay tray—the kind that fits underneath a large planter. Set 4–6 violets of complementing colors, in their own little pots, in the tray. Water weekly from the bottom & add a splash of leftover coffee to their drink. They will bloom happily for months. Violets, like me, love coffee. My friend Jan said that the acid in the coffee makes them flourish. I love these cheery flowers so much, I once vowed that if I ever had a little girl, I would name her Violet.

Buy one big bunch of blooms & distribute them in many little vases to spread color & cheer all around. Besides saving money, there's something so lighthearted about a tiny vase of flowers.

Sprinkle jellybeans around your Easter table.
The tiny ones look best.

Plant some spring bulbs during autumn in a place where no one will see them blooming. Then you won't mind cutting the flowers to bring indoors for bouquets.

salvation be exalted!
Psalm 18:46 (NLT)

I love the look of flowerpots with freshly turned soil. It seems that they're just waiting for something wonderful to happen.

69

EASTER
Assurance

We love Easter—baskets full of surprises, chocolate bunnies, egg hunts, daffodils and hyacinth dancing with the whispering breeze. But most significantly, Easter for us is the assurance that our faith is validated by historical truth.

It's a time when we remember that the creator of the universe came to earth as a man to suffer the pain and punishment of sins he did not commit. He paid the price for me, my sins, my inequities. And yours. Easter is a time when we try to grasp the awesome truth that the God of the universe loves us, personally.

Jesus said, "Greater love has no one than this, that he lay down his life for his friends." (John 15:13 NIV) Each one of us can be a friend of Jesus. He promised to prepare a place for us—"In my Father's house are many rooms; if it were not so, I would have told you. I am going there to prepare a place for you." (John 14:2 NIV)

He lives in heaven and, when we acknowledge the truth of what he did to save us, he promises that we will live with him there forever. Amazing. For me, this promise eases my fears. When my time here is over, I know where I'm going. Seeing Auntie Zorah and many others I have loved who have gone before me sounds wonderful.

So, celebrate Easter with complete assurance. Revel with family and friends in the immensity of God's love and mercy. Host an egg hunt. Plant flowers as you please. And be sure your destiny is sealed by calling on the One who has the power to seal it.

In my Easter bonnet with all the frills upon it...

I heard a loud shout from the throne, saying,
"Look, the home of God is now among his people!
He will live with them, and they will be his people.
God himself will be with them.
He will remove all of their sorrows, and there will
be no more death or sorrow or crying or pain.
For the old world and its evils
are gone forever."

Revelation 21:3-4 (NLT)

Hallelujah!
He is Risen!

Happy Hunting

Did you ever take part in a community Easter egg hunt when you were a kid? I did. I remember hundreds of eggs—pink, yellow, blue, green, and even shiny gold ones—hidden in the new grass, just waiting to be discovered. What joy!

The Furman family has hosted many hunts. To ensure that every child has a good time, we have developed a few guidelines. We've found over the years that these guidelines help ward off the blues often suffered by the more tentative hunters and the over-exuberant ones whose eggs bounce out of their baskets as soon as they're flung in.

For everyone who asks, receives.
Everyone who seeks, finds.
And the door is opened to everyone who knocks.

Luke 11:10 (NLT)

(The key is to ask and seek and knock!)

Easter Hunt Etiquette

Determine a maximum number of eggs allowed in each basket. Count all the eggs & divide by the number of kiddos participating.

Before declaring open season on the eggs, announce that each person may collect a certain number of eggs. We tell the hunters that when they've found that number, they should stop looking & enjoy their bounty. Make sure to tell the older children that they can help the little ones search if they'd like, but the little people should be allowed to pick up the eggs for themselves.

We like to vary the kinds of eggs in the hunt. We stuff some plastic eggs with candy or little toys. It's also fun to hide egg-shaped candy in nooks & crannies. (We find those all year long!)

Sometimes we put a star on a few eggs to make special prizes. Each kiddo may only have one of those. If an eagle-eyed hunter finds more, he can point them out to other kids. We try to have a special prize for every egg gatherer.

After Easter, if I'm really on the ball, I buy bunches of plastic eggs & toys on clearance & stash them away till the next year. It's always a pleasant surprise to open the decoration box & find the needed supplies already there. I must admit, though, I forget from one year to the next whether or not I bought more supplies. Opening that box is always a surprise.

When we have several families joining the fun, everyone pitches in to fill the eggs.

Tracey's Stuffed Mushrooms

I have an incredibly talented friend named Tracey. She does everything with flair. She's a terrific artist—I have one of her paintings in my bedroom. She is also an awesome interior decorator and cook.

When she gave me this recipe, she didn't specify the amount of each ingredient. Every time she makes these mushrooms, they're unique creations. (Like most experienced cooks, she creates by feel and not by recipe!) To find the right amounts, I had to experiment. Dave especially loves these, so he happily volunteered to be the quality control guy for each experiment.

Stuffed Mushrooms

35 – 40 large mushrooms
1 tsp. garlic, crushed
1/2 tsp. Worcestershire sauce
dash of Tabasco sauce (optional zing!)
2 Tbsp. olive oil

2 stems of green onions, finely chopped
1/2 c. Italian seasoned bread crumbs
1 egg
1 pint half-and-half
monterey jack cheese, shredded

Wash mushrooms & remove stems. Finely chop the stems then simmer them in a frying pan with garlic, Worcestershire sauce, Tabasco sauce, olive oil & onions. Fry until cooked through. (Real chefs call this "cooking until rendered.") Add breadcrumbs & egg & mix well. Stir to a paste consistency, adding olive oil if needed.

Preheat the oven to 425°. Spray a 13" x 9" glass baking pan with oil. Generously fill each mushroom cap with the paste mixture. Place stuffed mushrooms in rows in pan. Pour half-and-half into the bottom of the pan so that it comes halfway up the caps. Bake for 15-20 minutes. Sprinkle cheese on top & cook 10-15 minutes more. When the cheese has melted & browned slightly, they're done. I have stuffed the caps the night before I needed them & kept them covered in the fridge overnight. If you make them ahead of time, add the half-and-half just before putting them in the oven.

Serve piping hot & you'll soon find yourself with friends who are hopelessly devoted to you. Bon appétit!

Goes down so ssmmootthh... –Grandpa Glen

Rainy Day Blues Busters

How many times on a rainy day do you hear the whine of "Mom, I'm b-o-r-e-d!" Growing up in our house, mom would respond with "Only the boring are bored." Her wise words rarely failed to shake us out of our boredom blues. What kid wants to be boring? Of course, she also had on hand a list of boredom breakers to drive away the doldrums until the last drop dripped. Here are a few I now use with my boys:

• Play board games. The Furman Family is big on board games—there are so many life lessons lurking in every round. Here are a few of our favorites: Stratego, Parcheesi, Monopoly, Yatzee, Bible Trivia, Redemption Card Board Game, Checkers, Chess.

• Bake cookies. Did you notice the ricotta cookie recipe on this page? Why notta?

• Paint pictures. Watercolors wash up quickly and exercising your creativity can brighten up any gloomy guy. Don't stop at pictures-paint coffee filters for a spring flower bouquet, or make cards and bookmarks to brighten someone else's rainy day.

• Read books. This is one activity that can be done alone or in a group. Reading can take you on an adventure and you don't have to get wet!

• Put on a show.-Turn chairs over and drape with a blanket to make a stage. Act out a story or song or use puppets to entertain your friends and family.

• Go puddle jumping. Put on your old tennis shoes and shorts and jump from puddle to puddle seeing who can make the biggest splash. What kid (or grown-up) can resist?

• Have an indoor picnic. Spread a quilt on the kitchen floor and break out the basket. Add a few potted plants and play a tape with nature sounds to add atmosphere

• Rescue worms from the sidewalk. They go great in your garden. Don't be squeamish—save a worm today!

• Look for the rainbow. See who can spot the rainbow first

—Patricia Clifford

Ricotta Cookies

1/2 c. softened butter	1 egg	1/2 tsp. baking soda
1/4 c. ricotta cheese	1 c. sugar	1/4 sp. salt
1 tsp. vanilla	2 c. sifted flour	

Combine softened butter, ricotta & vanilla. Beat until creamy. Add egg & mix well. (For special occasions, add a few drops of food coloring, too!) Slowly pour in dry ingredients & blend until smooth. Spoon dollops of dough onto a greased cookie sheet. Bake at 350° for 10-12 minutes. Makes approximately 3 dozen cookies.

The work will wait while you show the child a rainbow, but the rainbow won't wait while you do the work.

Adventures with Dad

see who can swing the highest

Do something outdoors—almost anything will do

Every month or so Dave and one of the boys saunter out the door for special one-on-one time. Sometimes Dave lets the kids choose their destination. Sometimes they plot the adventure together. Often these outings are free or inexpensive. What is important is that dad and son spend time together, not that their activity is elaborate or expensive. In fact, it's obvious that our guys don't care a hill of beans where they go, as long as it is with their Daddy.

This time alone gives the kids a chance to share what's happening at school and with friends. It gives them an opportunity to express their feelings, concerns, and hopes privately to their dad. And it gives Dave a chance to impart his fatherly view of the world. There's no doubt in my mind, bonds that last a lifetime are woven together by times like these.

Dave started this tradition when the boys were tiny. Martin was just two. Along the way, there have been a few particularly busy months when we haven't been able to make time for these father-son outings. A funny thing happens, though. The kid who misses his time with Dad begins to show signs of, shall we say, moodiness. The symptoms are easy to recognize. Like Winnie the Pooh's friend Eeyore, he shuffles about with the attitude that life is like "a box of thistles," and he's been given "all the really tough and prickly ones." Suffice to say, we never have to keep track of whose turn it is. The boys let us know...one way or the other!

Go Sledding

Hunt for unusual rocks

fossils

& other treasures

Dig for fossils (matthew's 1st choice)

Go miniature golfing (one of micah's favorites)

Camp out overnight (martin's idea of a great time)

Treat your buddy to an ice cream cone

These commandments that I give you today are to be upon your hearts. Impress them on your children. Talk about them when you sit at home and when you walk along the road, when you lie down and when you get up.

Deuteronomy 6:6-7

Good Times

There is something very sacred about the undivided attention of a dad. A father's love can build up a young person in a way that prepares him or her for life as a devoted spouse and parent. At its best, a father's relationship with his child reflects the relationship our Heavenly Father wants to have with us.

When dad isn't available, however, a caring grandpa or trusted family member probably would feel honored to share special time with your young one.

Hike through the woods

Head to the playground & play pirate ship on the monkey bars

Browse through the library & then go out for a soda

Go to the pool & do splashy "cannonballs"

Go fishing

Buy a tube & bike tire & fix the flat

Mosey through a museum

Plan a trip to the workplace of someone who has a job your child thinks he'd like

Pack a picnic & find a quiet place

Pay up your insurance, don a pair of in-line skates & totter your way around the neighborhood—but don't forget the helmets & pads!

Walk the dog together

Go bowling & offer praise & encouragement at every opportunity

Surprise your kiddo with a trip to the store to buy a long awaited toy

Play tennis, basketball, soccer, —any sport your kiddo likes!

"Strike!" Go bowling

Play baseball

Go to a ballgame & splurge on funnel cakes

Take your little friend to a favorite restaurant

Ride bikes together

77

Amazing Strawberry Punch

The Springtime months are riddled with bridal and baby showers, birthday parties and Bible study groups, office parties and open houses! Any festive gathering that needs refreshments is the perfect place to serve this delicious punch.

1 10 oz. pkg. frozen sweetened strawberries
1 12 oz. can limeade concentrate
1 12 oz. can lemonade concentrate
2 2-liter bottles ginger ale
1 2-liter bottle seltzer
ice

Combine partially thawed strawberries & concentrates in blender & mix until smooth. Just before serving, pour ginger ale & seltzer into a large punch bowl. Add the concentrate mixture. Stir well, then add ice. Sweet, tart & refreshing! If you're throwing a big wingding, blend several batches & refrigerate them until you're ready to make the punch.

Eileen, the woman who gave me this recipe, is a friend from way back. Just after college, I was far from home and going through a difficult time. My buddy Robin and I were starting a graphics company. Eileen and her two grown sons were our favorite typesetters. They adopted me into their family. I spent countless hours over at their house. We went fishing, out to eat, and they typeset my class reunion yearbook for free. They probably didn't even know it at the time, but their friendship was better than therapy for me. Life is like that. Some little thing we say or do for people may have life-changing significance for them. And sometimes we don't even know the impact our thoughtful words or actions have had...until we get to heaven.

Here's a 'berry' good tip:

In a hurry and feeling punchy? (Pun intended!) Here's a quick and easy way to dress up any refreshment table:

Pick a pretty punch bowl and dump in a half-gallon of fruit sherbet (lime, raspberry, and pineapple—what's your favorite?). Over the sherbet pour cold lemon-lime soda, enough to fill the bowl. If you're feeling especially creative, toss in some chunks of frozen fruit (right out of the bag will do). Your spectacularly simple punch is ready to serve! Ridiculously simple and stunningly refreshing.

So encourage each other and build each other up, just as you are already doing.
1 Thessalonians 5:11 (NLT)

(Sounds like more than a suggestion!)

Picture-Perfect Parfait

This is such a simple recipe. It's inexpensive, light, and colorful, and our kids love it. Even Shrek's talking donkey knows everyone loves parfaits. It's a layer thing!

3-5 boxes of Jell-O, choose any flavors & colors you like in 3 oz. pkgs.
Whipped topping
Tall, clear parfait glass or vase with a wide top

Make the first package of Jell-O according to the directions on the box. Pour half of the gelatin mixture into the vase & leave the remaining half in the mixing bowl. Set both in the refrigerator. When the bowl of Jell-O has almost set, whip the gelatin until the color lightens & it becomes opaque. When the first layer has set completely, pour the whipped Jell-O on top of it to form the second layer. Spoon on a 1 inch layer of whipped cream to form the third layer & put the vase back into the fridge. Repeat this procedure for the remaining packages of Jell-O until the vase is full. If you can't find one large glass serving container, use tall clear glasses for each person & serve with iced teaspoons.

This dessert is sure to win rave reviews. Though, some say it's too pretty to eat.

Keeping the kids involved in the kitchen is key! Every time we include our children in the daily activities we are reassuring them that they are important and capable. We are also modeling for them what it is to be part of a family. For our parfaits we plan together which color should top the previous one. Then there are jiggle-testers to tell us when the jello is set and ready for the next layer. My boys love to use the handheld mixer to whip the Jell-o into a froth.

He has given us his very great and precious promises.
2 Peter 1:4

Uncle Fred's Ham

What a Hambone!

Uncle Fred is a gifted cook who tosses ingredients into a pot and wonderful meals emerge. We could not have Easter without Uncle Fred, Auntie April, and this magnificent ham!

1 c. brown sugar (sometimes Fred uses honey instead)

2 tsp. allspice

3/4 tsp. nutmeg

1 large can pineapple rings, reserve juice

1 can mandarin oranges (if the juice is necessary or desired)

1 large pre-cooked ham—we use turkey ham

Combine in a small pot the brown sugar, allspice, nutmeg & a cup or more of pineapple juice from the canned pineapples. Cook over medium heat until the mixture develops a light syrup consistency. If there isn't at least 1 cup of pineapple juice, strain the juice from a can of mandarin oranges. (It adds a fantastic flavor anyway!) Preheat oven to 350°. Set the ham in a large casserole dish. Pour warm sauce over ham but reserve some to pass around the table at dinner. Cover the casserole with a lid & cook for 1 hour. Remove lid & cook 1/2 hour more. Set pineapple rings across the top of the ham for the last 15 minutes to brown them slightly. Delicious!

"For I know the plans I have for you," declares the LORD, "plans to prosper you and not to harm you, plans to give you hope and a future. Then you will call upon me and come and pray to me, and I will listen to you. You will seek me and find me when you seek me with all your heart."

Jeremiah 29:11-13

Springtime Planting

The sweet fragrance of rich, wet dirt...the feel of a sturdy shovel in my hands...watching a tender seedling establish itself and take root...ahh, Spring!

A few years ago, the boys and I planted our first real garden. I have always been a gardening nut, but previously had planted mostly flowerbeds and container plants. This particular year was our first attempt at pumpkins, corn, and other veggies.

Uncle Fred selflessly tilled our stubborn soil five times. Finally, the red-brown clay relented and became pliable enough to shovel. Around that time, I saw a sign near our house offering free composted horse manure. Oh, happy day! I threw ten big black trash bags and a shovel in the trunk, and Micah and I ventured forth to claim a generous pile of manure for our own. After four trips, we finally had enough.

That year the fledgling family garden produced more than 40 pumpkins and enough corn for two big meals. The local black bear helped himself to some, too. After the harvest, I bound the dried corn stalks together and made a yard decoration for fall... which is actually why I planted corn in the first place!

Whenever I putter in the garden, I encourage the boys to help. I don't push it, though, because I'd like gardening to become as much a joy for them as it is for me. Most days at least one of the three boys will

May your roots go down deep into the soil of God's marvelous love. And may you have the power to understand, as all God's people should, how wide, how long, how high, and how deep his love really is.
Ephesians 3:17-18 (NLT)

stick with me for a while. One day we discovered an inquisitive but friendly garter snake exploring in the dirt. After much debate, we named him Nyoka, after the garden snake that tests the character of a young African girl in the book *Mufaro's Beautiful Daughters*. The boys were delighted also to find butterflies, praying mantis, ladybugs, and other critters doing business in our veggie patch.

In addition to food-bearing plants, we planted flowers. Now, every summer a climbing rose blossoms yellow and morning glory vines hang heavy with blue and pink flowers along the fence that divides our property. By early fall we have a row of bright sunflowers for the birds to nibble on.

To keep deer and other moochers from destroying our garden, we use a few eco-friendly techniques throughout the spring and summer. After the fall harvest, we invite our four-legged neighbors to hang around and snack on what's left.

One particularly successful strategy involves scattering freshly cut human hair all around the plants. I ask a nearby salon to save a pile for me. The hair deters most wild things, at least until it rains a couple of times. We apply new clippings every couple of weeks. Another helpful tactic involves marigolds. Just pluck off a few handfuls of marigold blossoms, drop them in a blender, and add water. Puree and then strain out the water. Squirt some dish soap into the strained water. Use a soap that's biodegradable, like Ivory®. Soap helps the liquid adhere to the plants and no one, four-legged or otherwise, wants a mouthful of soap! Pour the liquid in a spray bottle and mist the plants in the garden generously and often. Especially after a hard rain.

My mom has a lovely sign above her sink that reads, "Life began in a garden." I love that. In the hours I spend tending the garden, I pray and sing to the One who made the very first garden. What a blessing a garden is.

For MOM
Thumbprint Cookies

Pour the following ingredients into a zip top plastic bag:

3/4 c. brown sugar

1 c. flour

dash of salt

1/2 tsp. baking soda

2 Tbsp. cornstarch

1/2 c. chocolate chips

1/2 c. chopped pecans or walnuts

On a pretty card, print these instructions: mom's Thumbprint Cookies

1/2 c. soft butter or margarine   1 egg   1/4 tsp. vanilla

Combine butter, egg & vanilla in a bowl & mix until smooth. Add contents of bag & mix thoroughly. Pour batter into an 8" glass pan & bake at 350° for 20-30 minutes. When cool, cut into scrumptious, bite-size bars. Happy Mother's Day!

(If you're really strapped for time, fill the bag with packaged cookie mix. Then be sure to supply the necessary directions on the card.)

Save one empty tin can for every child making this Mother's Day gift. Tuck one bag of cookie mix into each clean, dry can. Next, cut a piece of light-colored card stock to fit around the can with a 1/4 inch overlap. Down the middle of the card, neatly print: mom's Thumbprint Cookies. make sure to leave the top & bottom of the card blank.

With an inkpad, help children put their thumbprints in the blank spaces of their can cover. Give them a quick demonstration of how to make pictures from their prints, and then turn them loose to decorate.

When they're finished, attach the card around the can with glue. I use a glue gun. Punch a hole in the recipe card, slip a ribbon through the hole, and tie the ribbon to the can. This is a terrific gift to make with your Sunday-schoolers on mother's Day.

mom's Thumbprint Cookies

1/2 c. soft butter or margarine

1 egg   1/4 tsp. vanilla

Combine butter, egg & vanilla in a bowl & mix until smooth. Add contents of bag & mix thoroughly. Pour batter into an 8" glass pan & bake at 350° for 20-30 minutes. When cool, cut into scrumptious, bite-size bars. Happy mother's Day!

> *"Be assured, if you walk with Him, look to Him, and expect help from Him, He will never fail you."*
>
> George Mueller

I sometimes can't believe that God has blessed us with three of the most wonderful little guys. The daily joy and laughter they bring into our home is immeasurable. Don't I sound like a doting mom? I know, I know! But those little ones entrusted to our care really do take the meaning of love to a new level.

Daily I pray that I will be the mother they need. Some days I even pray that God would protect them from me. When I hear myself yelling, being impatient, I think maybe I should be putting money aside for their future counseling sessions instead of for college! But, alas, God put them into our care, and I trust his judgment. He has me right where he wants me when it comes to this challenge of parenting. He has me on my knees, seeking answers and guidance. Motherhood is the hardest, most humbling job I have ever loved.

I am so thankful that there are places to turn for help on this wild and wonderful journey called parenting. Personally, I have really depended on the friendship I have had with other mothers. Women from my Bible study group, my neighborhood, and my family have blessed me over and over again with their prayers, advice, and concern. Thanks for being there for me, ladies!

Rebirth-days!

I like the idea of rebirth-day parties. The day you ask Christ to be Lord of your life is your rebirth-day. I heard of this remarkable tradition a few years ago, and since then, I've wanted to celebrate my kids' rebirth-days with our family. Only once have I even come close to it, though. So far, it's all I can do to host their other birthday parties! Still, their rebirth-day is a memory I want them to hold dear, so we've done a few other things to commemorate the occasion.

On each of their special days, I snapped pictures like a woman with a mission. Then I enlarged one & framed it. Those photos of the kids form a collage that hangs in our living room. On the back of each photo I recorded the details of their momentous step—where they were, what day it was, how old they were & who was with them when they prayed to become a child of God.

We keep a few new Bibles on hand in the hope that friends & family will open up their hearts to their Heavenly Father. Over the years, we've had the privilege of watching several kids & a few adults make that life-changing decision. To commemorate that step, I write all the pertinent information in the front of a new Bible. Sometimes we throw a celebration dinner for the new Christian & present the gift-wrapped Bible then. It's a thrill to give a gift that will help a new believer discover the true character of God & the promises he makes to his people.

On separate visits, our nieces Brittney & Olivia each asked to join God's family by inviting Christ into their hearts. When I was growing up, I never understood why my aunts and uncles loved us so much. Once my sisters started having babies, though, I understood what a joy it is to have nieces & nephews. To play a part in their spiritual growth is an honor & a blessing.

In the front of my prayer journal, I keep a list of nieces, nephews & others who I pray will come know Christ personally. It's so exciting when I can highlight a name & mark beside it the date that person accepted Christ's saving grace.

Olivia prayed the prayer and the angels celebrated!

Those Angels Had a Party!

Congratulations Brittney On Your Rebirthday I ♥ u! Aunt B♥

If you know the month in which a treasured friend committed her life to Christ, send a rebirth-day card. It will be an unexpected & welcomed reminder.

All honor to the God and Father of our Lord Jesus Christ, for it is by his boundless mercy that God has given us the privilege of being born again. Now we live with a wonderful expectation because Jesus Christ rose again from the dead.

1 Peter 1:3 (NLT)

"Cookie Pizza Please!"

When I asked Micah what recipe he wanted to share, he didn't hesitate—"Cookie Pizza, please!" Delicious and visually tasteful, this dessert will bring your guests back for more. Cookie Pizza is so easy to make, it's perfect for quick get-togethers, baby showers, and birthday parties. And it's special enough for Easter dessert.

Micah's Cookie Pizza

1 roll ready-made sugar cookie dough
1 8 oz. pkg. softened cream cheese
A variety of fruits that you love—raspberries, blackberries strawberries, blueberries, kiwi, mandarin oranges & bananas. Use lots of colors. Clean, peel & slice, then set aside.

Roll out the cookie dough into a large pizza shape. If you're feeling adventurous, cut it into a star or some other shape that fits the occasion. Bake according to the instructions on the package. Allow to cool, then spread softened cream cheese over entire cookie. Pile the sliced fruit on top of the cream cheese & serve. If you are using bananas, first dip them in orange juice so they won't brown as quickly. A treat for the eyes & sweetness for the taste buds!

So colorful and full of spring!

Micah, our youngest, is so easy-going. His first night home from the hospital, he slept through the night. That was a shocker for all of us, especially Grammy who had offered to hold him until he woke for his midnight feeding. I raced down the stairs at 5 a.m. and there they were—still rocking in the rocking chair!

Micah is friendly, funny, and very concerned that fairness prevails for everyone. A cuddly hug-bug, Micah hops in my lap at every opportunity. If I had to sum up my littlest guy, I would say, "He loves." Micah loves so many things—dominating Papa at dominoes, fishing with Grandpa Glen, playing Twinkle, Twinkle Little Star on the piano with Aunt Joy, reading to Grandma Dorothy, chasing butterflies, watching The Incredible Journey video, climbing Grandma BJ's mulberry tree, and of course playing with his big brothers. In truth, there are few things Micah doesn't love.

Children are a gift from the Lord; they are a reward from him.

Psalm 127:3 (NLT)

89

Special Delivery!
Hope for the Homeless

A few years ago we started a small mission tradition with our 5th-6th grade Sunday school class. Our goal was to get the kids to see how others struggle and encourage them to help even if only in a small way. Our 1-day excursion into the street jungles turned out to be a source of powerful lessons for all of us.

Here is how we did it.

In the weeks prior to the big delivery we talked about why a person might be homeless. Some reasons we listed:

Unemployment

Mental Illness

Veteran with special needs

Single moms (with small children especially)

Substance abuse

Lost hope

Disabled

Then we talked about what would be helpful in a "Goodie Bag" for a person living on the street. The kids were so insightful! I would never have thought of some of the ideas they presented. And it was moving to see kids who had probably never given much thought to the homeless really struggle with the concept that some people actually do not have a place to sleep at night.

Our brainstorming ideas:

Bible-(In an easy-to-read translation)

Bandana

Kleenex

Power bars

Hat

Phone card

Sunscreen

Lip Balm

Nuts

Water bottles

McDonald's gift certificates

Crackers

Gloves

Stamped envelopes

Pen and paper

Sandwiches

Carrot and celery sticks

Party mix

Toothbrush and paste

Tums

Before they went home that day, we read Mark 10:43: "But among you it should be quite different. Whoever wants to be a leader among you must be your servant, and whoever wants to be first must be the slave of all" (NLT). I asked the children to involve their families in putting together a sack or two for a homeless person, putting as many of the items in their bags as they could get and adding other items they might think of with their family. Our family contributed a few extras to make sure that every kid had a sack to give even if their own family wasn't able to participate.

pray without ceasing!

Party Mix

stay out from under bridges

When I explained our project, I got the Bibles at a reduced cost from our local Christian bookstore.

The next week in class we talked about what our afternoon mission trip might be like. The kids were aware that we could not anticipate the response each person might give—some would be thankful but others might actually get angry. But we decided that we were responsible for the spirit in which the gifts are given not what kind of reception they would receive.

Delivery Day! One sunny Sunday afternoon after church we gathered together in a circle to pray for our mission trip. We prayed for protection, boldness, opportunities to shine the Savior's love into the darkness. We lifted up the hearts of the folks we might meet and our hearts as well. We were sent off into the inner city bathed in prayer and hope. We felt invincible!

Teamwork was the name of this game! We made our strategy and we prayed some more. "Look your person in the eyes."

"Try to remember as much about them as you can—their clothes, their hair and eye color— so we can picture each person in our minds later and pray for him or her."

" When you hand them your bag say, "I made this for you. God bless you."

We delivered several bags on the way downtown. One kid would get his nerve up and shout, "I'm next!" and when we spied a person standing on a sidewalk holding a sign pleading for help we would pull over and the student and I would approach them together. Each gift was met with graciousness. When we got back into the van we would pray again for that person and watch them digging into the bag as we drove off.

Once downtown, we walked to a park that was home to many needy people. One of the first folks we encountered was a man passed out under a tree. He looked as though he had been in a fight. It was a startling observation for the kids. One of the boys insisted that he leave a bag near him so when he came to he would have something to eat and drink. I wondered aloud to them if when he woke up he might think angels had visited him. We prayed over him right there! The kids loved the idea of being someone's angel.

Afterwards, the kids agreed it was something they would like to do again and vowed to pray for their person for a long time. More than a year later, one of those kids who participated that day shared with me that she still prays for her blue-eyed person every day. Think of the impact that Allison's prayers are having on one homeless person's life.

Both my students and the folks we met seemed to be blessed by our adventure and I couldn't believe the impact it had on me! It's an opportunity that we plan to have again when our three boys are a little older.

Baskets of Kindness for May Day

Unexpected sweet surprises—what could be better? They're a thrill to give and a blessing to receive. May baskets are a cheery gift to make for someone in the spring. My kids love to tiptoe up to a porch, plunk down a basket, ring the bell, and run like the wind. Even my heart races as I watch from a hiding place. How gratifying it is to see the face of someone when he or she receives an unexpected basket of kindness.

If you don't have a spare basket to use, make one. Save one of the plastic green baskets that strawberries are packaged in. Shape a pipe cleaner into a basket handle and attach it to the carton. Cover the bottom of the basket with Easter grass or the real thing. Then tuck in a few chocolates, small flowers (lavender verbena or fragrant lilacs), scented candles, soap, lotion, and a tiny book of encouragement. Anything that will fit in the basket and make it more personal works.

Lotion

What a sweet surprise!

When planning your next sweet surprise, think of the office staff at your child's school, the librarian, babysitter, or someone who's lonely.

Catch a highway worker completely off guard & hand him (or her) an icy cold unopened soda...

Pay for the person behind you at a drive up window...Rake leaves in a neighbor's yard...

Where did our sense of community go? What happened to chatting over the fence, knowing the names of our neighbors, and congregating in the backyard for summer afternoon block parties? In many parts of our country, that feeling of neighborliness is gone. Perhaps if a few of us reach out, we can start a trend!

Write a few words of support to someone who is hurting.

Since God chose you to be the holy people whom he loves, you must clothe yourselves with tenderhearted mercy, kindness, humility, gentleness, and patience.

Colossians 3:12 (NLT)

Deliver a loaf of homemade bread & a bouquet from your garden to a newcomer...

93

Celebrating Summer

For the LORD God is a sun and shield;
The LORD bestows favor and honor; no good thing
does he withhold from those whose walk is blameless.

Psalm 84:11

Sunshiny, summer days—when the boys play happily on the hills behind our house till dinner, neighborhood ballgames spring up at a moment's notice, and pretzels, root beer, and ice cream are consumed in mass quantities. The summer sun brings sweaty, flushed faces, the familiar scent of sunscreen and lots of time to romp.

Most mornings, before the sun gets too hot, the boys and I putter in the garden. Under clear blue skies, we often gather at the fence to gab with neighbors we haven't seen since the weather turned. During the days, we spend many hours hiking, biking, pic- nicking & splashing in the pool. Sometimes, though, the boys and I just hang out, languidly reading, playing games & occasionally cleaning the house. In the evenings, we fire up the grill and ask friends to join us for backyard barbecues.

Fun summer days with cousins & friends.

One of the best things about summer is that the boys have time to play and just be kids. No pressures. No getting up early. No homework, scout meetings, or choir practices. The kids invite friends for day trips, sleepovers, sleep-outs and a few overnight road trips. Vacation Bible School gears up and piano practice, tight schedules and expectations gear down.

Summers are lived more in the open. Our windows are thrown open; our daily comings and goings are more in the open, too. It's a perfect time to shine for our Savior, though I sometimes fall short of being a shining example.

When our kids are playing with the neighbors, I often find myself teaching the delicate art of Backyard Squabble Mediation. While I don't relish these encounters, I know that they are valuable lessons for all the kids. Foibles and all, we're out there in the summertime.

More Lazy, Less Crazy!

Less laundry! Praise the Lord for that seasonal blessing. My theory is that shorts take up less space in the washer. At the Furman house, the kitchen also sees a little less action in the summer. Elaborate meals are few and far between when the days are hot and long.

One of our favorite summertime suppers consists of BLTs (bacon, lettuce & tomato sandwiches) made with turkey bacon. Cooking the bacon in the microwave makes this a simple, nutritious summertime meal completely prepared without heating up the kitchen. Slice a few fat, juicy tomatoes; add crispy fresh lettuce, a little mayo on lightly toasted whole wheat bread and you're good to go. Everyone, kids included, can create their own delicious combo. Add a slice of melon or some freshly washed bing cherries for a cool refreshing side dish.

Roll out those lazy, hazy, crazy days of summer. Those days of soda and pretzels, root beer.—Nat King Cole

The Wonder of Weddings

What's more common in June than June Bugs? Weddings!

I used to search and search for the perfect gift to commemorate each of these wonder-filled milestones. That is, until I thought up this inexpensive, much loved gift for the happy couple and their families.

Load your camera with black & white film. I use black & white film at every wedding, whether I give my photos as a gift or not. Few occasions photograph better in black & white than weddings. (It must be the contrasts—white gown, dark tux.) Look for classic moments—the groom dancing with his mom, the father of the bride hugging his grown up little girl, the flower girl dancing with the ring bearer, the newlyweds gazing into each other's eyes. Capture the close-up, personal stuff that characterizes the wedding and the folks attending. When I get the film developed, I ask for triple copies—one for the wedding gift, another to give away & one to keep. If I don't know the couple very well or if they really love photos, I keep the photos I like the best, then give all the rest away along with the negatives.

Pick a handful of the best shots & buy a multi-picture frame to display them in. Arrange the photos leaving one slot blank to write in the names, date & location of the event. Decorate around the pictures with colors from the wedding & write captions if you like. I often include a scripture verse too. On the back of the frame, write a note wishing the couple well. There you have it—a wedding gift for under $30! An added bonus is that you can give it to them after the wedding. This is good on two levels. First, you don't have to rush out beforehand to search the stores. And second, there's a chance you'll arrive with the perfect gift on the very day they realize the honeymoon has officially ended. Your present could bring a little perspective.

Colleen & Ben

The Bieshaar's

96

Wedding Guest to the Rescue!

For a little extra spending money, I used to make wedding cakes. Oh, could I tell you some wedding day stories! Now when I go to a wedding, I pack emergency supplies in a duffle bag and head out ready to respond to any distress signal.

In a frantic moment, have you ever had someone ask, "How can I help?" What a relief it is to find a willing soul in the middle of a crisis. And being the one to save the day is a blessing, too. So, next time you go to a wedding, pack a survival kit and let no job be too trivial. Put napkins on the tables, clean up behind the cake maker, or decorate the arch that was supposed to have arrived adorned with flowers and ready for show.

Wedding Survival Kit

snip, snip

- Extra pantyhose
- Static remover
- Extra shoes
- Exacto Knife
- Safety pins
- Hair spray
- Games & toys to entertain restless children
- Duct tape & transparent tape

- Cake serving Knife
- Lipstick & lip balm
- First aid Kit
- Glue gun
- Wire cutters
- Stain remover
- Food (nuts, candy, protein or granola bars—nothing messy)

- Extra film to share
- Scissors
- Wire
- Bobby Pins (white and brown)
- Clear Nail Polish (to stop those hose runners)

- Super Glue (to fix broken finger nails)
- Feminine products
- Batteries for your own camera & AA batteries to share

At every wedding I have been to, at least one of these items was desperately sought after. I love being able to say, "I have one of those!" What fun to be the one who comes through in a pinch. (But be prepared for the quizzical looks you'll get when they find out you carry around wire cutters and cake knives!)

A godly marriage is not created by finding a perfect, flawless person, but is created by allowing God's perfect love and acceptance to flow through one imperfect person you toward another imperfect person your mate.

Dennis Rainey

Love for a Lifetime!

In this age of soaring divorce rates, it is important to honor enduring marriages—like Dave's parents. Couples who have chosen to stand by their commitment through thick and thin are a priceless witness to how couples can love for a lifetime.

Display a framed photograph of the couple as newlyweds next to a recent photo of the anniversary couple. Or, present a collage of photos of the couple through the various stages of their life together. Ask guests to share when they first met the couple and one special memory. Today's reflections will be tomorrow's memories.

When Dave's folks were approaching their 50th wedding anniversary, Muff insisted she didn't want a big hoopla—just the family together to celebrate with them. But 50 years of marriage calls for a worthy tribute, so I decided to try what my friend Nancy did for her folks on their 40th anniversary. I gathered photos, stories, cards, and letters from long-time friends and family into a memory book and presented it to them on their golden day.

On the day of Mel & Muff's anniversary, their children and families gathered for a lovely dinner made by April & Fred. We presented the book of memories, and as soon as Mel & Muff saw the names of the contributors—some people whom they hadn't heard from for more than 40 years—tears began to flow.

Golden Memories

1 year in advance

Remind the children of the couple (& any other invited guests) of the big anniversary. Ask everyone to set aside that special day for a celebration in honor of the couple. If you are able, offer to help with travel or accommodations.

Just before the gala
make a gift tag for the book

To: Mel and Muff in Celebration of Half-A-Century of marriage
From: List all the names of those who contributed to the book

8 months in advance

Devise a scheme to acquire the couple's address book for a few hours without them knowing it. Photocopy all the pages, then write a letter to all their friends.

Give folks a due date of 6 months before the actual anniversary. You'll be amazed at the wonderful things that start appearing in your mailbox!

6 months in advance

Assemble pictures of the "bride & groom," their children & grandchildren, their homes, accomplishments, kids graduating...any photos that help tell the story of their life. I happened upon a few of their baby pictures & a few of them when they were first dating at Allegany College. If you can find one of their wedding invitations, include it too. Press flowers of the same variety & colors they had in their wedding to use in the decorating of the book.

4 months in advance

To get an idea of the general layout, put the book together without fastening the pics down. I organized the entries chronologically. The anniversary cards I compiled at the end of the book.

3 months in advance

Send a reminder postcard to those who haven't responded to your letter. Suggest that they send material within 2 weeks, so that they can be assured it will be included in the book. Make sure your phone, address & email information are clearly visible. Begin decorating the memory book.

1 month in advance

Arrange a time & place to hold the celebration & compile the guest list. Plan the dinner or finger food. If possible, surprise your honorees with at least one person they will not expect. Finish the memory book, leaving a few blank pages for late arrivals & photos of the celebration.

A Sample Letter

Hi!

In a few short months, mel and muff Furman will be celebrating 50 years of marriage. To mark their achievement, we're secretly creating a book chronicling their life together.

Today we're writing in the hope that you will share your memories of mel and muff. We'd like to collect your comments on an 8" x 10" page that can be mounted in a special album. Photos, funny or meaningful stories, and small mementos that represent their journey through life will make this book a real treasure. If possible, please write only on the front of your page so that we can use glue on the back. Also, please label your photos with the date, identities, and description of what's going on in the picture. (Sticky notes work great for this.) If you attended mel and muff's wedding and wouldn't mind parting with a few of your photos from that occasion, we'd sure love to have those, too.

In order to allow enough time to compile the material, we need to have your contributions by December 10, 1997.

Thank you for your kind consideration. Your efforts are sure to be deeply appreciated by mel and muff.

Sincerely,
Dave & Liz Furman

P.S. I've sent this letter to everyone in mel and muff's address book, so I realize that some of you may not know the honorees on a personal level. To all of you dentists, hairdressers, plumbers, etc., please don't feel obligated to respond.

Love never gives up, never loses faith, is always hopeful, and endures through every circumstance.
1 Corinthians 13:7 (NLT)

The Power of One

My mom, Grandma BJ, is a creative chef. After my parents divorced, I think she became even more resourceful, and watching her use her ingenuity has been a very valuable lesson for me. In fact, through all the trials, mom taught me many lessons about how to face adversity with honor, determination, and hard work.

Single-handedly rearing four teenage daughters while working full-time as an emergency room nurse, my mom selflessly loved us. By her example, we learned that loving someone sometimes means sacrificing your own needs. As my sisters Paula, Jane, Jennifer & I were growing up, mom also taught us to tow the line and contribute to the running of the household. She cautioned us about the pitfalls of pride and held us accountable for our choices. With endless encouragement, mom pushed us to be all that we could be and prepared us for the challenges life inevitably presents.

My sisters and I consider mom one of our closest advisors and friends. I pray that someday my own children will love me to the depth that I love her.

Grandma BJ's Strawberry Shortcake

Shortcake ingredients~

2 1/3 c. Bisquick® baking mix

3 Tbsp. white sugar

3 Tbsp. margarine or butter, melted

Preheat the oven to 425° & grease an 8" x 8" pan. In a bowl, combine Bisquick®, 3 Tbsp. sugar & margarine, then mix until a soft dough forms. Pour dough into pan. Bake 15-20 minutes or until golden brown. Cut into squares.

Topping ingredients—

6 c. sliced strawberries
1/4 c. white sugar
1/2 gallon lime sherbet
whipped cream

In a bowl, pour 1/4 cup white sugar over sliced strawberries & stir to coat thoroughly. To get the flavor flowing, crush the berries a bit while you're mixing. Cover the bowl & refrigerate until serving time.

When it's time for dessert, place a square of shortcake on a plate. Top with a generous scoop of lime sherbet & 1 cup of strawberries. Add a dollop of whipped cream & prepare your taste buds for a yummy summer treat. Serves about 6.

Lip Smackin'   *Good!*

Too short on time for shortcake?

I sometimes have to remind myself that dessert can be something as simple as slices of watermelon, chunks of cantaloupe or honeydew melon, or whatever fresh fruit is in season. Juicy & packed with natural vitamins & nutrients, a fruit dessert is cool and light. Yum! Simple desserts can look elegant with little effort— serve in a pretty dish or stemware, garnish with a sprig of fresh peppermint, or add a fancy butter cookie.

*We can do no great things,
only small things with
great love.*

mother Teresa

Father's Day Feast

A few years ago on Father's Day, Martin (who was nine at the time) decided to create a special dining experience for Daddy. He transformed the house into "The Father's Inn." He printed a menu on the computer and decorated around the print. The good dishes were pulled out and Martin set the table impeccably. With very little help from me, Martin made the entire meal. Then, when it was time to eat, we were instructed to go outside and enter as if it were a real restaurant.

Whenever we dine out, Dave's standard order is "three cheese enchiladas." So that is what Martin decided to make. He also baked a three-berry pie, tossed a salad, and made Spanish rice to complement the enchiladas. Dave was very touched by this special evening and it was a great experience for Martin. He even cleaned up the mess (with very little prompting).

Martin's Cheese Enchiladas

1 pkg. whole-wheat tortillas
1 15 oz. can enchilada sauce—hot, medium, or mild
3-4 c. grated mild cheddar cheese
1 chopped tomato

1/2 head lettuce, chopped
sour cream
guacamole
1 small onion, diced

Spray a 13"x9" pan with oil. (Martin recommends a glass pan.) Pour 1/2 cup of enchilada sauce in the bottom of the pan & spread around. Lay a tortilla on a clean surface & sprinkle cheese down the middle. Roll up & place in the pan. Repeat until pan is full. Pour remaining sauce over the top of all the enchiladas & sprinkle more cheese on top. Bake at 350° until cheese melts. Serve with chopped lettuce, tomatoes, sour cream, guacamole & diced onions. A great dish for Dad.

Dig in!

A mom's love makes them strong!

102

Our prayers make them strong!

Martin, our oldest son, loves anything to do with science and has an affection for snakes and spiders that I am only beginning to appreciate. When he was very little, he claimed that he wanted to be a "bugologist" when he grows up. By the time pre-kindergarten graduation rolled around, he announced to the audience, "When I grow up I want to be an entomologist, an artist, and a snake biologist." His college years are still quite a way off, but we're willing to speculate he'll choose a career in science.

The depth of Martin's character amazes me. Not long ago, he organized a party for a boy in his class who was moving. He feared the boy felt that no one cared if he left. When someone is sick or upset, Martin is quick to compose his thoughts in a card or letter of encouragement. And it is often Martin who leads us in prayer when a crisis arises.

One fall I asked Martin what sport he wanted to try that season. His reply was, "Mom, I really want to take piano lessons. I'll skip a sport so it won't cost so much." He is still taking piano lessons and adding trumpet next year. He also has taken up basketball.

Ingredients for making a hero

Our children will be tomorrow's heroes if we invest in their character today. The one thing above all that will mold our young men and women into heroes is a consistent, earnest walk with the Savior. Their 'hero-ness' may not be revealed until a time of testing, but if you are building the characteristics listed below into your children, you have a hero in the making.

Faith	Patience	Kindness	Self-control
Joy	Honesty	Gentleness	Independence
Peace	Integrity	Selflessness	Responsibility

Our children will not always display these characteristics—after all, they have us as their teachers! But we can be intentional in choosing activities, family traditions, and relationships that will encourage these traits. Why not choose a characteristic a week to work on together as a family? Post a definition and talk together about what it will look like in the lives of each family member. Encourage each other in your walk.

You don't raise heroes, you raise sons.
And if you treat them like sons,
they'll turn out to be heroes, even
if it is just in your own eyes.

Walter M. Schirra, Sr.

our heroes!

It's a mom thing!

Feasting in the Great Outdoors

Whenever possible in the summer months, our family moves the food outside! To accomplish this feat we require all hands on deck. Load a few trays, platters, or bowls with things like the silverware, condiments, glasses and napkins. Stick with unbreakables if you have little ones.

Just like in the story of the Little Red Hen, anyone who wants to partake in the breaking of the bread must join in the carrying of the trays (both before and after dinner). The kids don't mind because they love to "eat out." Our back porch becomes a hubbub of activity and laughter as we eat. At every dinner Dave asks each child what he did during the day. Many an unresolved problem has been solved over the barbeque chicken. On occasion, our feast is shared with a neighbor passing by or an impromptu invitation is issued to family or friends who happen to drop in. These unplanned gatherings build special memories. I love summer!

A few years ago, our former assistant pastor mic and his wife Phyl moved out of town. I was lower than a snake's belly when they left. However, along with a great many heartwarming and funny memories, they left us with two fabulous lime recipes. One warm summer afternoon they served us lime chicken for lunch, and I remember the fragrance of it grilling set my mouth to watering.

Lime-Lite Chicken

Pucker up!

Lime shouts of summer & this simple recipe is not only refreshing, but also gratifyingly low-fat.

4-5 chicken breasts (boneless & skinless)	1 c. lime juice 3-4 cloves minced garlic	Salt & pepper to taste

marinate thawed chicken in lime juice, garlic, salt & pepper for 1-2 hours in the refrigerator. Pour off juice & grill until cooked through. Cut into slices & serve on a huge salad. This chicken is so tasty, it can easily pose as an elegant entrèe. Pair with wild rice & steamed veggies & you've got a lovely, healthy meal.

Quick Lime Pie

Smooth as glass!

2 large graham cracker pie crusts

1 large pkg. lime Jell-O

1/2 gallon premium vanilla ice cream

1 lime, sliced

Whipped cream

Using only 1/2 the water called for on the Jell-O package, heat the Jell-O in a pan. When it has dissolved, remove from heat & spoon in ice cream. Stir until smooth. Pour into pie crusts & refrigerate. For a bit of grandstanding, top with whipped cream & slivers of lime. To save time on party day, prepare the night before & refrigerate. A quick version of a cool classic.

Grill Skills

Even though summer rolls around every year, I can never seem to remember how to properly clean the grill! For those of you who, like me, suffer from grill-cleaning amnesia, here are a few tips to keep handy:

Gas Grill

After the food is finished cooking and off the grill, turn the grill on high heat and close the lid. In about ten minutes all the marinades and food chunks stuck to the grill will be turned to a fine white ash. Turn the grill off, let it cool a few minutes and scrape with a wire brush. By cleaning the grill after each use, you'll not only be ready to roll for next time but removing the delicious remnants will help keep the bears, raccoons, and other critters from investigating.

Charcoal Grill

After cooking but while the grill is still hot, scrape any food or marinade remains from the cooking surfaces with a long-handled wire brush. After the grill has completely cooled, dispose of all charcoal ash. If you lined your grill with foil when it was new, dispose of the foil and ash and reline your grill with clean foil. This keeps cleanup to a minimum. The removable racks in small grills can even be washed in the dishwasher after scraping.

Smells delicious!

A Few Safety Tips: make grills off-limits to children. On gas grills, keep the lid open after turning on the gas and before lighting so gas doesn't accumulate.

Use long-handled matches or propane lighters to light grills. Only use charcoal lighter fluid before lighting. NEVER stand over a grill while lighting and NEVER leave a grill unattended.

So whether you eat or drink or whatever you do, do it all for the glory of God. 1 Corinthians 10:31

105

Old-Fashioned 4th of July

Every year we trek to Mel and Muff's Black Bear Country Inn in Dubois, Wyoming, to take part in the 4th of July fanfare of small town America. A community of only a few more than 1,000 hearty souls, Dubois is situated between the Wind River Indian Reservation and Togwotee Pass in western Wyoming. Eagles soar overhead through the crisp mountain air. Moose and bear meander through neighborhoods. And the townsfolk go all out when it comes to throwing a patriotic celebration.

Every 4th of July there's an enthusiastic parade through town and a rubber-ducky race down Horse Creek. After all the excitement from that has died down, family, friends, and guests of the Black Bear Country Inn congregate for a cookout down by the river near the inn. With full tummies and full hearts, folks sit and chat and wait for nightfall, when a fireworks display showers the hills above the town. As the time between dinner and fireworks draws to a close, we serve ice cream cones to all interested guests and friends. My boys love to take orders for flavors and serve the crowd.

Our visit to Dubois for the 4th has been a tradition for more than a decade. Through the years, we've become fast friends with visitors from all over the world, honeymooners, and the local pastor and his family, including 12 children at last count. (So far, they've adopted 10.) The friendships we've forged and the fun times we've had we'll treasure forever.

When I was a kid, we slurped on red, white & blue bomb pops every 4th of July. To me, those popsicles are as much a part of the birthday of America as fireworks. Ahhh, traditions!

With malice toward none; with charity for all; with firmness in the right, as God gives us to see the right, let us strive on to finish the work we are in; to bind up the nation's wounds, to care for him who shall have borne the battle, and for his widow and his orphan—to do all which may achieve and cherish a just and lasting peace among ourselves and with all nations.

Abraham Lincoln

"What? No potato salad?"

Dave's mom, Mary-Ethel Furman (affectionately known as Muff), is a Proverbs 31 woman. As a devoted spouse to her husband and a loving parent to her three children, she has lived in the same God-honoring way as the woman in that Bible passage. Muff, we rise up and call you blessed!

One year Muff concluded that no one would notice if she didn't make her potato salad. At our annual 4th of July picnic, everyone was busy setting out the provisions, when suddenly Dave's keen powers of observation detected an important element was missing. "We forgot the potato salad!" he exclaimed with alarm. "Could somebody run up and grab it from the fridge?"

As gently as I could, I broke the news to him that Muff had opted not to make it. Dave was grief stricken. Muff knew then just how wrong she had been. Everyone missed her famous, original, time-honored potato salad.

The following year when we pulled into Dubois for our annual show of patriotism, our van was stocked with 10 pounds of potatoes and a dozen eggs to "help with the shopping" and ensure that Muff's potato salad made it to dinner. Isn't it funny how food traditions are some of our most anticipated? Family recipes offer more than flavor and a few calories, they're packed with memories, too.

Muff's Original 4th of July Potato Salad
(For a crowd or just Dave)

10 lbs. of potatoes, peeled, boiled, cooled & diced

3 large white onions, finely diced

1 large bunch of celery, diced

1 doz. eggs—hard-boiled, cooled, shelled & diced

salt & pepper to taste

2 c. mayonnaise

1/2 c. vinegar

1/4 c. sugar

a pinch of celery seed & dill to taste

Mix potatoes, onions, celery, eggs, salt & pepper in a large bowl. Seal with a cover & set aside. In a separate bowl, blend together the mayonnaise, vinegar & sugar. Pour the sauce over the potato mixture & stir until potatoes are well coated. Sprinkle with celery seed & dill, if desired. Refrigerate overnight or until chilled.

Charm is deceptive, and beauty does not last; but a woman who fears the LORD will be greatly praised. Reward her for all she has done. Let her deeds publicly declare her praise.
Proverbs 31:30–31 (NLT)

Your Undercarriage Will Sparkle! Sparkle!

After the tragic events of 9-11, I felt compelled to show my patriotism in some way. It seemed most everybody in the area had the same thought. By the time I got to the store, there wasn't a single flag remaining. So for the first time in my life, I ventured bravely into cyberspace to search for and buy a magnetic flag to display on our van. I accomplished this feat in record time and when the much-sought-after purchase arrived, I was thrilled. Emblazoned across the magnetic sign was the American flag and underneath were the words "God Bless America." Perfect.

The first few times I drove around town with the sign on the car, I would look in my rearview mirror to see if the car behind me noticed my cool magnet. I felt I was making a statement "I believe in this country and the freedom for which it stands!" However, the very first time I took the van through the "touch-free" carwash, I forgot to take my new flag off and it was washed away. UGH!

When I realized my show of patriotism had slipped off, I knew it had to be on the floor of the car wash. So the next morning, Micah, Matthew and I stopped by the car wash on our way to drop Martin at choir. As we pulled up a gentleman was about to enter and the door to the bay was slowly opening. Seizing the moment, I jumped from the van and dashed toward his window. I politely asked if I could sprint in ahead of him and retrieve my little flag. He waved me on enthusiastically.

I waited for the door to open and entered the bay. As I entered, the little electric eye must have caught sight of me. In an instant the undercarriage wash came on with such startling force that I was airborne before I knew what had hit me. A flying leap took me through the spray and when I landed the pre-rinse immediately opened up, drenching me from head to toe. Without looking at the man in his car behind me, I escaped as fast as I could with no flag to show for my troubles.

The howls of laughter rocking my van told me that Matthew and Micah had witnessed the entire show. As I crawled behind the wheel of the van, icicles forming on my brow, I couldn't help but share in the laughter. Despite my frozen exterior, joining in the hilarity with my boys warmed my heart! But I'm not sure if the man who treated me to his car wash ever recovered.

It's a Grand Old Flag, It's a High-Flying Flag

In late September of 2002, the American Legion had an article in the "Rocky Mountain News" to remind us of proper flag etiquette. The Webelos of Boy Scout Pack 625 distributed copies of these guidelines around the neighborhoods. It was obvious that few folks (including myself) had any training on how to properly display our nation's flag. Here are a few of those guidelines so you can fly our flag proudly:

Fly Old Glory anytime between sunrise and sunset. After dark, only fly her if properly illuminated.

Never fly the flag with stars down, except as a distress signal.

The flag should never be used as a costume or uniform.

Never let the flag touch the ground or carry it horizontally or use it as a drapery, covering or receptacle.

Hoist the flag briskly, lower it ceremoniously.

When flying the flag at half-staff, any other flags on adjacent poles should also be lowered to half-staff or removed.

For flags that cannot be displayed at half-staff (such as a house or porch set), attach a black streamer to the top of the pole, allowing the streamer to fall naturally.

A flag mounted on a wall or in a window also cannot be displayed at half-staff. A black bow knot either with or without streamers should be placed at the fastening points.

Window display: Hang the flag vertically with the blue field to the left of someone viewing it from outside.

Other flags can be displayed beneath the American flag at half-staff from the same pole if there is adequate room; otherwise the others should be removed.

Life is not a laughing matter—but can you imagine having to live without laughing?

Leonid Sukhorukov, Laughing matters

Oohh! FIREWORKS!

Rambling Road Trips

Once the boys become old enough—at least old enough to look around—we figure they're ready to travel the open road. Rambling 'round the country-side, visiting family & friends, seeing the sights, we cherish these times of togetherness and adventure.

No matter where we go, we always come back with stories. We love to recount the adventures we've had at parks along the way. There's a park in Fort Collins, Colorado, built to resemble a castle. It has tall wooden turrets, swaying bridges, and even a drawbridge to play dragons and knights and fair-haired princesses. (That's me.)

Some of our memories are full of fun; some are memories of when we took the wrong turn, ran out of gas, and nothing worked out the way we planned. And some stories have become family legends. Like the night Martin's asthma flared up while we drove over a dark mountain pass. As he gasped for air, we careened through a snowstorm, frantically searching for an electrical outlet to use the nebulizer, a device that allows him to inhale medication and breathe freely. We ended up in the back office of a McDonalds. As Dave and I sat shaking in fear with Martin, the employees treated the kids to Happy Meal toys and lots of attention.

The fear that came over me when Martin couldn't breath was indescribable. As parents, it's almost unbearable for us to watch our children suffer. I would have gladly taken the place of my hurting child, if I could have. I wonder if that is how Christ felt when he offered to bear the painful consequences of our sins. Because of his sacrifice, we don't have to endure the pain of eternal separation from God. Instead, we spend eternity in his house. What a loving Father he is.

Greater love has no one than this, that he lay down his life for his friends.

John 15:13

Travel Tips

I love road trips!

Buy a bag of pipe cleaners & a How to Make Cool Stuff with Pipe Cleaners book. My Kids will contently twist and bend and create cool thingamajigs for hours as I drive. If you can't find a How to book, give the Kids a few of every color & let them make their own creations.

For long trips, gift wrap some new little toys & fun snacks. Dole them out to the gang one at a time. I bring three of each surprise, so every Kid gets to open each surprise.

Are we there yet?

A small trash can, moist wipes, tissues & a first aid Kit are must-haves in the car. Those few items have saved us more than once.

Pack a lidded box with colored pencils (they don't melt) & drawing pads.

Have the Kids draw postcards to send to their buddies back home. If your Kids can't write, have them dictate to you. Be sure to bring your address book & stamps so you can mail them along the way.

Hi Carol,
Today we saw a bear! Wish you were here.
DL3 ms

Carol

Glorious Gorp!

Make a gorp with snacks that are fun to munch & easy to vacuum—pretzels, Kid cereals, raisins & other dried fruit, m&ms, cheese crackers, & any dry finger food your Kids love. We Keep a lidded plastic jug of gorp in the car for road trips & everyday hunger pang emergencies.

When the sun's beating on the windows, towels & receiving blankets are great to use as sunshades. Just anchor one end of the towel at the top of the window & voila! Everyone travels in cool comfort. Sometimes our sunshades are also used to clean up spills. Very handy.

WATER

Buy a 24-pack of bottled water in case of thirst attacks. This simple strategy silenced the relentless pleading to stop & buy drinks. We're saving money & time, the boys aren't drinking the sugary stuff & if we have a spill, WHO CARES!

Are we there yet?

Look! A park! Can we stop?

Making Tracks

Legend:
- ★ Dave
- ★ Liz
- ☆ Martin
- ★ Matthew
- ★ Micah

I want to go to the beach!

The boys came up with a fun way to track our travels. We purchased a big map of the United States and mounted it on a bulletin board. We also purchased colored star stickers in various colors. Every family member chose a favorite color star, and that became the one color that person uses to mark his journeys.

After we visit a state, each person gets to put his star on that state. (I thought about marking each state that we travel to as a family, but as the kids get older, they may travel without the whole entourage.) Martin wanted his own map to color so I made a few extras—one for him and enough for his brothers too.

Dave and I would like to visit as many places as we can. In fact, I would love to take our boys to all 50 states before they turn 18, but I doubt that will happen. I haven't been to all 50 states, and I'm a tad beyond the age of 18. Dave and I believe that traveling and seeing how others live opens young minds to new perspectives. Even within our own borders, there are so many different cultures. Experiencing God's many different creations is awe-inspiring.

As a child, Dave and his family camped across the country. And some of my funniest childhood memories involve family vacations. Many of our ventures were short trips, which might seem insignificant, but they weren't to us kids. As a special treat, once each semester, my mom took us out of school for a family field trip. We went to museums, factories, national parks, and historic sites. The best thing was having a mom so cool that she would let us skip school to spend the day exploring with her.

Life is a great big canvas; throw all the paint on it you can.
Danny Kaye

A day full of fun!

On those long lazy days of summer I have many times pulled out these three recipes that I collected during my years of teaching Kindergarten.

Play Dough

1 c. flour	2 teaspoons food coloring
1/2 c. salt	1 tablespoon oil
2 tablespoons cream of tartar	
1 c. water	

Mix the first three ingredients together in a medium pot, then combine and add remaining ingredients over medium heat stirring constantly. After 3-5 minutes, the mixture will form a ball. Remove from pan and knead for 2-3 minutes. Store in tightly closed container in refrigerator. (Optional: Adding a few drops of flavoring such as vanilla or almond will give it a wonderful scent as well.)

Bubbles to Blow

1/3 c. dish soap or baby shampoo	1 and 1/4 c. water
2 teaspoons sugar	Optional: 1 drop food coloring

Mix together all ingredients and store in an unbreakable bottle. Experiment making bubbles with all sorts of kitchen gadgetry like slotted serving spoons, straws, little green strawberry baskets, tea brewing ball with the holes, pipe cleaners made into shapes, soda pop plastic connectors and any other thing you can come up with. Do not drink!

Shaving Cream Fun!

If you have a smooth-topped table outdoors (not wooden), squirt huge globs of shaving cream on the top and turn the kids loose. They can write names, draw pictures with a finger pencil, or make foamy sculptures. No table? Give each child a cookie sheet with cream instead. You will be amazed at how long they will be entertained! When the fun is over, spray down the table (and for fun, the kids) with the hose for an easy clean up. The table and the kids will be cleaner than ever before. (Caution: avoid cream with menthol which can irritate skin and eyes.)

Family Reunion Fun!

One year, a rash of funerals and a few weddings brought the extended family together several times within a few months. Though the occasions were rather draining emotionally, we enjoyed being together so much that, by about the third occasion, most of us were saying, "Why wait till the next time somebody gives up the ghost or gets hitched? Let's have a reunion!" Aunt Phoebe and Uncle Woody took that sentiment to heart and orchestrated the first family reunion ever for my Dad's side of the family. It was a SMASHING SUCCESS, so I thought I'd share a few of their ideas.

First, send a postcard, well in advance of the gathering, asking everyone to keep the date of the reunion open. Promise to follow up with details several months before the reunion. Try not to plan your get-together on a holiday weekend, unless it is a little celebrated one.

Pick a location that is easy to reach & you'll have a higher turn out. Send a map. Check to make sure there are places to camp & motels close by, in case some folks want to make a weekend of it. Provide information on those as well.

Plan your party with a theme... Phoebe & Woody chose A Family Garden. Phoebe made a giant family "tree" to put by the entrance where everyone signed in & got their nametags.

Nametags are a MUST, especially for those of us a little weak in the upper story! I bought visors for all the kids & made colorful computer labels of their names to stick on the brims. The kids also needed nametags, though, because they took the hats off immediately after receiving them. (Of course!)

If this is your first reunion, start small. A lunchtime gathering will help foster good vibes among the kin with cold feet. Once they see how fun it is, they'll jump at the chance to go to the next get-together.

Phoebe & Woody had our event catered. (And I did my level best to make sure there were no leftovers.) Everyone pitched in for the catering, but to save money, a potluck would work beautifully too.

At our reunion, there was a planting activity for the kids. I bought lots of pots at garage sales, enough so that every kid could plant petunias & marigolds to take home. While we planted, I talked to the group about how families are like plants. With nurturing attention, families & petunias bloom happily their whole lives.

Ask a relative who can write well to compose a brief history of the family's matriarch & patriarch. My sister Paula read a biography of Grandpa Glen & Grandma Gladys (my Dad's parents) who started this branch of the family tree.

If you can find reasonably priced t-shirts, have a few printed with the family name & reunion celebration date. They make great door prizes. Or, if you're feeling flush, buy one for everyone who plans to attend.

Set up a table with photos collected from high & low. We also had a sign up sheet for those who wanted copies of a few pictures of Grandma & Pa.

Ask a well-spoken relative to emcee the event. Uncle Woody kept the ball rolling for us & his son Mark video-taped all the action.

If you are the planner of a family reunion, don't forget to give a token of appreciation to everyone who helped. My Aunt Liz presented me with a set of dishtowels she lovingly embroidered herself.

Ask as many family members as you can to help plan & participate in the activities. You may not be able to tell just by looking at them, but Phoebe & Woody are of shrewd & nimble minds. They knew that everyone who had a job to do would have to come to the event. (Not that anyone needed to be tricked into attending!) Some relatives manned the check-in table, some were asked to lead us in prayer, some were in charge of researching the family history & compiling the info into a packet to hand out to everyone. And some were asked to judge the "Draw Grandma Contest."

Compile one address book per family with everyone's addresses, phone numbers & email information.

If you are helping someone orchestrate a reunion, it's a nice touch to give them a gift & recognize their efforts. I was so occupied with the activities of the day, that I didn't think of a thank-you gift until it was too late. I regret that.

Set aside time for folks to share memories of their growing up years. Everyone shed a few tears during our sharing time. There's something about recounting family history that draws us closer together.

For each table at our reunion meal, I made centerpieces with sunny yellow mums. After lunch, my cousin drew names & each person whose name was drawn won a centerpiece to take home.

Give prizes to the one who traveled the farthest, stayed married the longest, produced the most grandkids, lost the most hair & is the most recently married. (At our get-together, a cousin convinced her new spouse to stop by on their honeymoon. Those of us with a few years of marriage under our belts came to the conclusion that any spouse willing to make that kind of sacrifice on his honeymoon has a good chance of staying hitched forever.)

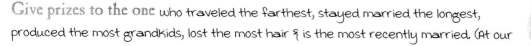

"This is your life..."

After the reunion lunch, Phoebe & Woody surprised my Dad with a commemoration of his life. He's the only male of the Cowen family left, and they wanted to honor him. Everyone regaled us with funny memories, shared their appreciation for him, and read letters from people he attended high school with. At the end of the roast, my three little guys read a poem to him and presented him with a framed copy. It was quite a lengthy tale, but here's a snippet—

Grandpa Glen &
Grandma Dorothy

Fishing Grandpa

We have a fishing grandpa
that we love to go and see.
He lives right near a lake that
has some fish as big as me.
Grandpa teaches lots of things
from his own backyard
Like riggin' up our poles before we go
and hit it hard.
While we sit patiently for fish to bite our
poles and bait,
Grandpa sings us silly songs and
rhymes to help us wait.

116

Our families are like the soil that supports, nourishes and

Sharing Our Faith 101

When it comes to opening my mouth to share the Good News sometimes I find I have lock jaw. I'm afraid of saying the wrong thing and offending someone. Or, that I'll be asked tough questions I can't answer. Or, that they may know me well enough to know that my life is not always a reflection of the life-change God is doing in me.

But then I also feel guilty for not sharing—for not telling about all the blessings God has brought into my life. So, here's the deal! I've decided not to force people to listen to my story if they're not interested. But if the subject comes up, I want to be ready to simply tell how much my faith means to me. No fancy rehearsed speech or litany of memorized answers—just plain and simple.

What will I say? I will just tell them that the God of the Universe loves me and has taken me into His care. That He has given me a peace I had never known before I asked Jesus to rule my life. And that I can trust Him to make everything in my life work out for my good. But the best part is that God loves them too and wants them to know a peace beyond understanding. All they have to do is ask. Guaranteed.

That's my story and I'm sticking to it!

No God, No Peace. Know God, Know Peace.

Still when Woody & Phoebe called and asked me to share my faith & open the festivities of our family reunion with a prayer, I was apprehensive. I don't know where most of my relatives stand on spiritual matters. Person to person is one thing but up in front of my whole extended family is quite another.

Shortly after they asked me, however, the horrible tragedy occurred at Columbine High School. Micah & I were in the park right next to Columbine when the shooting began. We heard the explosions, got on our knees & prayed as ambulance sirens screamed all around us. When I got home, news came over the prayer chain that nine children from our church were still unaccounted for. Thankfully, all were found safe some time later. The waiting, however, was excruciating. The church across the street from ours, however, lost several members that day. Our whole community was heartbroken.

Suddenly, I wanted desperately to share my faith with my family. No one knows when we will draw our last breath. The reunion could be my one and only chance to share with my family what I've discovered to be true about our Lord and Savior. Nowhere can we find true peace and hope, but in Him. How could I not share my faith with some of the people I love most?

So, I encourage you to step out in faith, even when it is not easy. Ask God to give you His words. This news is so good, it must be shared. Once you have told what you have found in Him, He will do the rest.

encourages each plant to reach, grow and blossom.

Bunches of Broccoli Salad

When my sister came to visit from Maine a few summers ago, she and her husband Brad made us a meal we still talk about. Brad cooked a whole turkey on our little kettle grill and Jane made this great salad she got from her friend Diane.

2-3 large bunches of broccoli

12 slices turkey bacon cooked & crumbled

1/2 medium onion, finely diced

1/2 c. roasted salted sunflower seeds

1 c. miracle whip® (not real mayonnaise)

1/2 c. sugar

2 Tbsp. red wine vinegar

Wash and cut florets to small bite-sized pieces & set aside in a large bowl. In small bowl, mix together miracle whip®, sugar & red wine vinegar. Pour mixture over broccoli & stir to coat thoroughly. Cover & refrigerate for at least 5 hours. I usually make it the night before. Just before serving, add the sunflower seeds & bacon.

The first time I walked into a Wal-mart and found my sister Jane's books on the shelf, I handed them to every passing shopper. moms, infants, businessmen—I wanted everyone in the store to have a copy of Baby Angels. I was so proud of her. Not only is she a talented author and illustrator, she's also someone who offers me a fresh perspective on the sticky situations I seem to get myself into. Jane is the kind of woman who calls things as she sees them. There's something very reassuring about that. And, whether or not I'm ready to accept her perspective, I can always count on her steadfast support and encouragement.

Sibling Rivalry

In my family growing up, we had four girls very close in age. Oh, the war stories I could tell you! Most of the time mom handled everything well, but occasionally our bickering ad nauseum would send her over the edge. Now as a mother of three boys, I know how she felt! Even though my sisters and I survived our battles, when our boys fight it drives me crazy. I just can't watch the kids I love trying to tear each other apart. And trying to referee? Forget it!

I know the experts say that healthy sibling rivalry usually grows into strong adult friendships, but you still have to survive the early years at home. Here are a few tips that have helped ease the struggle in our home.

When Martin, our oldest, was tiny I read somewhere that when you are expecting a new baby you should try to make up words to a little song telling how great friends they will be. I did that and sang it at bedtime and in the car a lot. They would often ask me to sing the Brother Song. Still today, though for the older ones it has to be the right time, I sing the song I made up for them. Here are the words to a stanza and the chorus. It helps to be reminded that friends will come and go but your family is forever.

The Brother Song

Chorus:
Martin, Matthew, Micah are brothers
Best Buddies they always will be.
They'll shoot hoops and play games together
And be best buddies you'll see.

And then when they get a little older
Off to pre-k they will go
They'll learn their letters and paint bright pictures
And have so much fun don't you know.

We talk around the dinner table sometimes about how great it is going to be to each have two friends they can count on in life. When they have troubles, they can share them, when great things happen, they have someone to celebrate with. And then they watch us with our own siblings.

I tell them the story of how as a 7th grader I got beat up by an 8th grader. My two older sisters came to my rescue. They love that story and ask me to tell it over and over again. Grammie tells of how she, in defense of her twin brother, came home from school after a fight. Her brother told his mom to make her quit saving him as it was just plain embarrassing to have the bully beat up by his sister. We take advantage of every chance we get to reinforce their friendship. Still, sometimes there are fights. In our house if they fight over a toy, the toy goes into time out for the rest of the day. They hate this rule so much that many a fight has been spared (and many a toy has been timed out too).

Hang 'em up!

Bighearted Blessings

Remember what it's like to move to a new place? An endless sea of brown boxes, an aching back, frazzled children, and no toilet paper anywhere. To top it off, it's practically impossible to cook in all the pandemonium, even if you weren't dog-tired. Believe me, there's no better way to welcome new neighbors than to show up on their doorstep with food.

I also include a card with our names and phone number on it and invite the new neighbors to call us if they need anything. One mom who had recently moved told me that when her son got sick in the middle of the night, she frantically searched the phone book trying to find the closest hospital. What a comfort to have at least one name and phone number of someone who has lived in the area awhile.

Chocolate Chip Banana Bread

1/2 c. shortening
1 c. sugar
2 eggs
2 c. flour

1 tsp. soda
1 tsp. salt
1 c. mashed ripe bananas
1/2 c. nuts, optional

1/2 c. chocolate chips (this is my contribution to the recipe)
1 Tbsp. cinnamon sugar

Preheat oven to 350°. Prepare a bread pan by greasing & lightly flouring it. Cream together the shortening, sugar & eggs, then stir in the mashed bananas. Set aside. Sift the flour, soda & salt together into a separate bowl. Gradually add sifted ingredients to the creamed mixture & blend well. Fold in nuts & chocolate chips, if desired. Pour mixture into 9"x5" bread pan & bake at 350 <degrees> for 1 hour or until done. (To test for doneness, insert a toothpick into the center of the loaf. If it comes out clean, with no crumbs stuck to it, the loaf is ready.) I got this recipe from some wonderful former kindergarten students Michael & Aaron. This was their great grandma's recipe, she sprinkles cinnamon sugar over the top of the loaf before it's baked. That's the best part!

And do not forget to do good and to share with others, for with such sacrifices God is pleased.
Hebrews 13:16

Welcome Someone New into the Neighborhood

We lived in a condo for many years and had several opportunities to serve as goodwill ambassadors. Though it pains me to admit it, there have been instances in which days (okay, weeks) passed before we made our first appearance at the newcomers' home. Nevertheless, we were always warmly received...no matter how long it took us to get over there.

Kids are great icebreakers and our boys love to deliver the goodies. I try to have as many items as I have carriers, so every member of our welcoming committee gets to deliver one gift.

Gifts to Share!

A pie

Phonebooks

A houseplant

Pumpkin bread

Cupcakes or a cake

Produce from the garden

A neighborhood directory

A seasonal wreath or spray

A plate of cheese and crackers

Freshly cut flowers from the garden

An invitation to pizza dinner at your house

Chocolate chip banana bread (see recipe to left)

A map of the neighborhood with store locations and hours.

A box of doughnuts and a pot of coffee or juice on their moving day.

A plant for their yard (I often take starts from my garden plants to give)

A Moving Day Survival Kit

How about this housewarming gift for someone you love...

Any combination of these and others you can think of would probably be greatly appreciated! Picture hangers, tacks, small nails, spackle, a razor blade scrapper, air freshener, toilet paper, power bars, a six pack of their favorite sodas, paper towels and spray cleaner, paper cups and plates, a hammer, a few clean dry rags, heavy garden gloves, a roll or two of pretty shelf liner, gunk off or fingernail polish remover to remove stickers etc, a favorite tape or CD to listen to while moving in, A fresh batch of homemade cookies, scratch removing marker.

Nobody made a greater mistake than he who did nothing because he could do only a little.

British Statesman Edmund Burke, 1756

Another survival kit! I'm big on surviving!

It Took a Village...

and all the help the Lord sent to create this book. I am also positive I will forget to mention someone who helped in a big way. But that doesn't mean I'm any less grateful! So here's to the nearly endless list of folks who were dedicated prayer warriors, cheerleaders, frustration-absorbers, sounding boards, entertainers of children (ours!) and just generally helpful:

Ken & Molly Bieshar (parent-like encouragers)

Brad & Harumi Makato & Tim Butler

Mike & Cay Carroll (encouragers)

Bruce, Lisa, Allison, Roslyn and Bryan Cole

Pastor Duane Cory and Pastor Neal Browne (awesome teachers!)

Tim, Stephanie & Steven DeWitt

Dave & Verleen, Erin, Josiah & Alyssa Didier

Our Deer Creek Church Family (many as close as blood kin)

DCC's 2001 5-6th Grade Sunday School Class (many of whom prayed daily for me and this project!)

Deer Creek Church's Prayer Chain (who took this project on as their own, praying me out of many a jam)

My Women's Bible Study Group (gifts from God, each one)

Greg, Molly, Daniel & Harry Frauenhoff

Danny, Charlene, Aubree, Jacob, Joshua, & Alana Gevara

Shirley Gonerka (who encouraged by reading my first chapter before I gave it to the editors because I was fearful)

Linda Heesh (who gave me money to go to the Colorado Christian Writer's Conference even though I didn't tell her I needed the money. It was at the Conference that Janet Lee picked up the book! God is great!)

Amy Keller

Chris & Kim, Sam & Molly Mc Callum

Pastor Don and Lorna McPeck (extreme prayer warriors!)

Brian & Brenda, Will & Austin Robinson

The Staff at Roxborough Elementary School(who cheered us on through the whole long process of publishing)

Mary Rouse & Carin Hansen

Trish & Bill, Ben, Drew & Jordan Schlitzer

Jan & Steve Sperry (willing ear, editor, cheerleader, prayer captain, cattle prodder, sitter, recipe tester, writing buddy and first editor. Jan was among the first to edit my stuff!)

Paul Thalos

Tom & Jean, Kara & Ben Stewart, our godchildren (all four are huge helpers!!)

Mark & Aletia, Danny & Vonda Westlake

Elizabeth Kain, Ron & Nethanial Zaik

My Sisters and their families:

Paula & John, Brice, Seth & Sean (The Cowbells)

Jane & Brad, Jo & Freeman Cowen Fletcher

Jennifer & Jeff, Brittney, Olivia, Jake & Emily Meyers

Dave's Brother and Sister & their families:

Dr. Wayne & Jane, Kristin & Jonathan Furman

Fred & April Struck & daughter Carol Brumfield

My moms and Dads

B.J. Cowen (what can I say-MOM says it all!)

Glen and Dorothy Cowen (Cheerleaders!)

Mel and Muff Furman (Muff took over my kitchen so I could write and paint this book. What a huge job cooking for 7 every night! She is a dear! Mel played endless games of dominoes with the boys to occupy them while I painted and wrote!)

Dave's Aunt and Uncle

Uncle Dick & Aunt Joy Wilsted (who while on a visit here during my final deadline entertained the boys during their break from school!)

My Aunts and Uncles (who prayed this book into existence)

Aunt Liz & Uncle Ted Siedenburg

Aunt Joan & Uncle Bill Starnes

Aunt Phoebe & Uncle Woody Wood

Praying Cousins everywhere too numerous to name but very appreciated!

The Douglas County Library Workers (from the book mobile who tirelessly searched for photographs for me of every imaginable object as fodder for my sketches!)

Peg Hooper (Librarian and childhood friend)

Cheryl Brian, Mary Ellen Gormican, Gail Moyson,

Penelope Powell, Lori Sanchez, Pat Sanchez, Diana Schmidt

Dr. Ali Eslaminia and Staff (who came to the rescue of my aching back when it went out in the 11th hour)

The Staff at Cook who are so talented and kind and allowed this dream to actually happen:

Janet Lee (project manager, talented editor and woman with great vision!)

Jeff Barnes (art expert and art director)

Julee Bate (editor, recipe tester, word fixer, babysitter, cheerleader, and friend extraordinaire)

Helen Harrison, contract art director, Ya Ye Design (art whiz, problem fixer and dream molder)

Ann Harjes (scheduling wizard and great juggler)

Kim Brandon (who took over as scheduling wizard when Ann left)

Michele Tennesen and Dione Russell (without whom you would probably not be reading this)

Eric Weber, photographer

Skow Photography (for letting me use the boys' school pictures in this book)

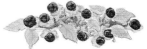

The folks listed below graciously allowed me to share their recipes & ideas with you. Some contributed old family recipes, some shared ideas they invented, and the origins of some contributions remain a mystery.

Fall

Quick Apple Crisp—Muff Furman

Lunch Box Ideas—The Didiers, Dr. Jean Stewart, Martin, Matthew & Micah

Crab Cakes—Mary Ellen Covino

Butterscotch Crunchies—Cañon City Junior High Home Economics Teacher

Porcupines—Verleen Didier

Basket Pass Idea—Covinos

Broiled Turkey Sandwiches—Jerry Berry

Turkey Enchiladas—Lorri Berry

Winter

Fruity Cookies and Vanilla Wafer Date Cookies— Great Auntie Zorah Jones

Holiday Wreath Cookies—Matthew Furman

Peach Spiced Tea—Great Auntie Zorah Jones

Cave Manger Design—B.J. Cowen

Eggnog—Jane Furman

Pecan Pie from Heaven—Hippo Bakery

Caramel Cinnamon Rolls—Sharon Pittman

Box Topper Ideas—Janet Lee

Handprint Hugs—Jane Cowen Fletcher

Spring

Stuffed Mushrooms—Tracey Matthews

Amazing Strawberry Punch—Eileen Penner

Easter Ham—Uncle Fred Struck

Thumbprint Cookies for Mom—Lorri Berry made these with her Sunday School Class with a different recipe but the idea was hers.

Adventures with Dad—Dave Furman

Cookie Pizza—Micah Furman (with help from Tammi Kackak)

Summer

Lime Lite Chicken—Phyl Cain

Quick Key Lime Pie—Phyl Cain

Great Grandma's Banana Bread Recipe—Rob, Michael & Aaron Rizzuto

4th of July Potato Salad—Muff Furman

Strawberry Shortcake—B.J. Cowen

Wedding Memory Book—Nancy Medberry

Flag Etiquette—American Legion

Family Reunion Productions—Woody and Phoebe Wood

Cheese Enchilada—Martin Furman

Broccoli Salad—Diane Rochford

A Personal Note from the Author

I always dreamed that as an adult my family life would be like living in an updated Walton's farmhouse with grandma and pa living in the back bedroom. I pictured lots of kids, pets and bedrooms and a big country kitchen with everyone gathered around the long wooden table.

What I had pictured all those years and the reality of family life for Dave and me is dramatically different. In our first dozen years of marriage and beyond, we have lived in a condo that Dave's parents graciously rented to us. No garden, no horses, no goats, and neighbors right behind the wall. This condo was a beauty, and surprisingly big too, but not a farm.

It pains me to admit it but for the first six years of that time I made no effort to fix up the place, to meet the neighbors, to plant perennials, nothing. I prayed often during those years for peace about the place we were living in until one day I looked into the eyes of our oldest son, Martin, and realized that he was growing up. He did not share my dream of the big, old farmhouse yet he was just blooming where he had been planted.

I'm not sure what changed but I am certain that it was not the living arrangement. Once I stopped waiting for the right circumstance, the place I was in became right. I got to work painting the inside of the condo and fixing it up a little at a time as we could afford it. I found I had great peace. I even found a spot to plant a garden that produced over forty pumpkins the first year we planted it! And I realized I did not need a big, old farm to make life magic for our family.

A few years later, the Lord opened doors for me to write this book. Who knew? Someone recently asked me if I was another Martha Stewart because I was writing this book. I laughed, as I thought of Laundry Mountain rising up from the floor in my basement and the wild herds of dust bunnies in the bedrooms upstairs. I wonder, would they still be impressed if they heard me hollering at the kids for bickering? Let me set the record straight. My kids' library books are often late. Our tiny backyard has been destroyed by our puppies. Dave and I argue (imagine that)! But I also know that a family is a treasure beyond measure and that wherever you are can be home. It turns out my mom was right all those years ago when she encouraged us to bloom wherever God planted us. Okay sprouts, start bloomin'.

Craft & Idea Index

  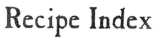 

Recipe Index

Verse & Quote Index by Text

If you have enjoyed this book, or if it has impacted your life,
we would like to hear from you.

Please contact us at:

Honor Books
Mail Station 244
4050 Lee Vance View
Colorado Springs, CO 80918

Or visit us at:

www.honorbooks.com